THESE ARE MY RIVERS

Books by Lawrence Ferlinghetti

POETRY

Pictures of the Gone World
A Coney Island of the Mind
Starting from San Francisco
The Secret Meaning of Things
Back Roads to Far Places
Open Eye, Open Heart
Who Are We Now?
Northwest Ecolog
Landscapes of Living & Dying
A Trip to Italy and France
European Poems & Transitions
Wild Dreams of a New Beginning
A Far Rockaway of the Heart

PROSE

Her (novel)
Tyrannus Nix?
The Mexican Night
Love in the Days of Rage (novel)

PLAYS

Unfair Arguments with Existence
Routines

TRANSLATION

Paroles by Jacques Prévert
Roman Poems by Pier Paolo Pasolini

LAWRENCE FERLINGHETTI

THESE ARE MY RIVERS

NEW & SELECTED POEMS

1955–1993

A NEW DIRECTIONS BOOK

811
FER

Manufactured in the United States of America
New Directions Books are printed on acid-free paper
First published clothbound in 1993
First published as New Directions Paperbook 787 in 1994
Published simultaneously in Canada by Penguin Books Canada Limited

The publisher acknowledges the following publications in which some of the poems in the "New Poems" section of this book first appeared:
AB Bookman's Weekly (1992) "Triumph of the Postmodern"; *City Lights Review* (1988) "Uses of Poetry" and (1989) "Avioncitos"; Fantome Press (1990) "Ascending over Ohio"; *Long Shot* (1991) "Sherman's March Reglitterized"; Spotlight Press (1987) "The Canticle of Jack Kerouac"; *Trap* (1988) "Poet as Fisherman"; *WPFW 89.3 Poetry Anthology*, Bunny and Crocodile Press (1992) "I Genitori Perduti"; *Zyzzyva* (1990) "Report on a Happening in North Beach, San Francisco."

In addition to new poems, the poetry included in this book has been selected from the following: *Pictures of the Gone World* (City Lights, 1955); *A Coney Island of the Mind* (New Directions, 1958); *Starting from San Francisco* (ND, 1961); *The Secret Meaning of Things* (ND, 1968); *Back Roads to Far Places* (ND, 1971); *Open Eye, Open Heart* (ND, 1973); *Who Are We Now?* (ND, 1976); *Northwest Ecolog* (City Lights, 1978); *Landscapes of Living & Dying* (ND, 1979); *Endless Life* (ND, 1981); *European Poems & Transitions* (ND, 1984).

Library of Congress Cataloging-in-Publication Data
Ferlinghetti, Lawrence.
    These are my rivers : new & selected poems / Lawrence
Ferlinghetti.
308 p.   cm.
    Includes index.
      ISBN 0–8112–1252–1
      ISBN 0–8112–1273–4 (pbk.)
      I. Title.
PS3511.E557T48   1993
811'.54—dc20   93–10383
                                                                              CIP

New Directions Books are published for James Laughlin
by New Directions Publishing Corporation
80 Eighth Avenue, New York, 10011

THIRD PRINTING

CONTENTS

for
various brothers & lovers
eternally present

Ho ripassato
le epoche
della mia vita

Questi sono
i miei fiumi . . .

[I have revisited
the ages
of my life

These are
my rivers . . .]

—GIUSEPPE UNGARETTI

NEW POEMS

A BUDDHA IN THE WOODPILE

If there had been only
one Buddhist in the woodpile
In Waco Texas
to teach us how to sit still
one saffron Buddhist in the back rooms
just one Tibetan lama
just one Taoist
just one Zen
just one Thomas Merton Trappist
just one saint in the wilderness
of Waco USA
If there had been only one
calm little Gandhi
in a white sheet or suit
one not-so-silent partner
who at the last moment shouted *Wait*
If there had been just one
majority of one
in the lotus position
in the inner sanctum
who bowed his shaved head to the
Chief of All Police
and raised his hands in a mudra
and chanted the Great Paramita Sutra
the Diamond Sutra
the Lotus Sutra
If there had somehow been
just one Gandhian spinner
with Brian Willson at the gates of the White House
at the Gates of Eden
then it wouldn't have been
Vietnam once again
and its "One two three four
What're we waitin' for?"
If one single ray of the light

of the Dalai Lama
when he visited this land
had penetrated somehow
the Land of the Brave
where the lion never
lies down with the lamb—
But not a glimmer got through
The Security screened it out
screened out the Buddha
and his not-so-crazy wisdom
If only in the land of Sam Houston
if only in the land of the Alamo
if only in Wacoland USA
if only in Reno
if only on CNN CBS NBC
one had comprehended
one single syllable
of the Gautama Buddha
of the young Siddhartha
one single whisper of
Gandhi's spinning wheel
one lost syllable
of Martin Luther King
or of the Early Christians
or of Mother Teresa
or Thoreau or Whitman or Allen Ginsberg
or of the millions in America tuned to them
If the inner ears of the inner sanctums
had only been half open
to any vibrations except
those of the national security state
and had only been attuned
to the sound of one hand clapping
and not one hand punching
Then that sick cult and its children
might still be breathing
the free American air
of the First Amendment

USES OF POETRY

So what is the use of poetry these days
What use is it What good is it
these days and nights in the Age of Autogeddon
in which poetry is what has been paved over
to make a freeway for armies of the night
as in that palm paradiso just north of Nicaragua
where promises made in the plazas
will be betrayed in the back country
or in the so-green fields
of the Concord Naval Weapons Station
where armed trains run over green protesters
where poetry is made important by its absence
the absence of birds in a summer landscape
the lack of love in a bed at midnight
or lack of light at high noon in high places
For even bad poetry has relevance
for what it does not say
for what it leaves out
Yes what of the sun streaming down
in the meshes of morning
what of white nights and mouths of desire
lips saying Lulu Lulu over and over
and all things born with wings that sing
and far far cries upon a beach at nightfall
and light that ever was on land and sea
and caverns measured out by man
where once the sacred rivers ran
near cities by the sea
through which we walk and wander absently
astounded constantly
by the mad spectacle of existence
and all these talking animals on wheels
heroes and heroines with a thousand eyes
with bent hearts and hidden oversouls
with no more myths to call their own

constantly astounded as I am still
by these bare-faced bipeds in clothes
these stand-up tragedians
pale idols in the night streets
trance-dancers in the dust of the Last Waltz
in this time of gridlock Autogeddon
where the voice of the poet still sounds distantly
the voice of the Fourth Person Singular
the voice within the voice of the turtle
the face behind the face of the race
a book of light at night
the very voice of life as Whitman heard it
a wild soft laughter
(ah but to free it still
from the word-processor of the mind!)
And I am a reporter for a newspaper
on another planet
come to file a down-to-earth story
of the What When Where How and Why
of this astounding life down here
and of the strange clowns in control of it
the curious clowns in control of it
with hands upon the windowsills
of dread demonic mills
casting their own dark shadows
into the earth's great shadow
in the end of time unseen
in the supreme hashish of our dream

POET AS FISHERMAN

As I grow older I perceive
Life has its tail in its mouth
and other poets other painters
are no longer any kind of competition
It's the sky that's the challenge
the sky that still needs deciphering
even as astronomers strain to hear it
with their huge electric ears
the sky that whispers to us constantly
the final secrets of the universe
the sky that breathes in and out
as if it were the inside of a mouth
of the cosmos
the sky that is the land's edge also
and the sea's edge also
the sky with its many voices and no god
the sky that engulfs a sea of sound
and echoes it back to us
as in a wave against a seawall
Whole poems whole dictionaries
rolled up in a thunderclap
And every sunset an action painting
and every cloud a book of shadows
through which wildly fly
the vowels of birds about to cry
And the sky is clear to the fisherman
even if overcast
He sees it for what it is:
a mirror of the sea
about to fall on him
in his wood boat on the dark horizon
We have to think of him as the poet
forever face to face with old reality
where no birds fly before a storm
And he knows what's coming down

before the dawn
and he's his own best lookout
listening for the sound of the universe
and singing out his sightings
of the land of the living

MATISSE AT THE MODERN, MAGRITTE AT THE MET

It is November nineteen ninety-two
and the Matisse Dancers
are dancing their dance at the Modern
on fifty-third street Manhattan
still ecstatic and speechless and
oblivious to all
except themselves and their own
private music
even as they are changed by the bright
American light
And it is not the first time they've changed
as they danced on through the century
these pale French country dancers who
turned pale red
when they went to St. Petersburg
While here now in Manhattan
the hard white sky washes over them
And here now is Matisse himself
here's Matisse at eighty
rolling around in his wheelchair
wheeling about through the retrospective
of his whole life
surrounded by more beautiful bourgeois
models
than he had ever dreamed of
and they almost pirouette around him
like extras in his troupe of Dancers
And they have come to see the dream of themselves
in paint
and he is heir to the Impressionists
and he gives them his impression
light as air
He does not question their existence
He merely reaches for his scissors

and cuts up a couple
to paste up on his walls
back home
And he continues to cruise about
through the hundreds of
Upper East Side ladies
all looking at themselves
on the walls
And the lovelies in the paintings
with birds nested in their eyes
look out upon these later versions
of themselves
coming and going in the rooms
of the Modern
And the disasters of painting
in which disaster abounds
has no sight of them
Meanwhile up the Avenue
and only a dove's flight away
here's Magritte at the Metropolitan
here's Magritte the surreal subversive
co-opted in spite of himself
Magritte the Communist insurgent
disguised in derby and topcoat
as a proper Belgian bourgeois
Magritte the camouflage artist
the photo copier
the collagist
in paint
who claimed he was not a painter
but painted
the visible behind the visible
and let others name it
and camouflaged only himself
in derby and topcoat
He who fell in love with the Invisible
and spent his whole life escaping

the bourgeois vision of reality
(as Matisse saw it
as Matisse embodied it)
He with the false mirrors for eyes
in which was reflected
the unimaginable the inexplicable
the unspeakable unconscious
the impossible seen as a distinct
possibility
He who every time he picked up a paintbrush
questioned everything
As in "The Human Condition" seen in a landscape
through the window of
a landscape on canvas
in which the painting represents
exactly what is hidden by the canvas
As in the "Clairvoyance" of the painter
looking hard at an egg
and painting a bird in flight
And "The Lovers" with their heads in shrouds
attempting to kiss each other
through the awful cloth
Next to a red-haired nude à la Matisse
who is almost fingering a pebble nipple
her tongue about to lick her own shoulder
and her other hand upon her vulva
in an auto-erotic parody
And a Black Flag hung
in the melancholy mystery
of a street at midnight
And "The Weariness of Living" of a man and a woman
taking off into the air in different directions
from a dinner table with the
white tablecloth of ennui
Next to the painter himself
seeing himself as a "Sorcerer"
seated at table eating & drinking

11

with four hands
And the painter himself "Attempting the Impossible"
painting a nude standing next to him
(not in or on a canvas)
the tip of his brush on her real arm
painting it in
Next to a naked woman whose left side
is made of the man embracing her
Next to a pair of naked feet
made into a pair of shoes
with laces through the skin
a possible future mutation
And "Heraclitus's Bridge" with
a dense white cloud hiding half of it
so that the bridge looks like it reaches
only halfway across the river
in which however is reflected
the whole bridge
and the whole scene contradicting
or not contradicting
Heraclitus the famous
Weeping Philosopher
who wept aloud because
the passing impressions of living
lead to a false idea
of the permanence of
the external world
Next to the impermanence of a tombstone
inscribed with a year
far in the future
While the "Discovery of Fire" ignites a
cool tuba
And "Elective Affinities" are embodied in
a single egg
about to become a bird whose tricks
will be frustrated by the painter
Next to a Greek god-like man reclining
with an erect woman for a penis

And three candles curled like snakes on a beach
                    their heads upraised and burning
Next to "The Unexpected Answer" of an almost
                                    human hole in a
                        bedroom door which
                may throw some light
                            on the darkness within
Next to a wall of building-blocks
            with four of them spelling out
                        REVE
                and the whole construction called
                    "The Art of Conversation"
While a rhinocerus climbs
                    an upright Roman column
Next to four or five men eating each other
                            in a "Famine"
Next to "The Survivor" a single old rifle
Next to "Youth Illustrated"
                    in a lost green landscape with
            a long long road winding through it
                along which at various distances
                    spaced across the years
                        can be seen in retrospect
            a bed a boy's bicycle a real lion an armless
            plaster bust a barrel and other
                    earlier memories too distant
                            to be recognized
Next to our "Intimate Friend" himself in derby
        with his back to us looking out
            upon a wilderness far away
                and the huge hard rock of his
                                dreamed reality
            poised on a windowsill about to
                            crush the dreamer
Who himself ends up at last inside
        an actual life-size bronze coffin sculpture
                sitting on a
                        Récamier chaise

the coffin bent up in the middle
as if the invisible corpse
were sitting upright in it
in a last covert attempt
to subvert the dominant paradigm

TRIUMPH OF THE POSTMODERN

The violins tended to shriek
escaping their linear melodies
The symphony band in running shoes
tapped out tunes from MTV
and poets deconstructed themselves on NEA grants
and joined linguistics departments
as others (baffled into silence)
took to the hills chanting sawmill haikus
or opened up unisex hair parlors in Des Moines

You're so minimal!
cried studio-mates to each other
doing DeKooning in Day-glo
(perversive not subversive—
art an ice-cream cone about to melt down)
Not to worry my dear
The maid can clean it up—

And Mother 'married' the Count
of the Lower East Side
as it used to be called
as *he* used to be called
before he opened that Gallery
so Uptown my dear
a huge disaster darling
the kind that makes millions
and he did he did
on the Tokyo Exchange
'My *girl*-friend painted them'
boasted the painter himself on-camera
raking in the shekels
with his diamond-paste tiara
(He'd been tri-panned in the Sixties)

Awesome! cried the cricket critics
and ever since it's been *dolce vita* except

the *dolce*'s on the dry side
like certain lower Italian dessert wines
nobody drinks anymore

And 'The point of the painting
is the point'
another painter kept explaining
imperfectly aware that saying *that*
meant nothing at all
which was the point after all
before things got so metaphysical
like Dolores with his pants down
flying down to Rio for a Drag Queen *Festa*
(except it all happened
at The Dakota)
My dear he trilled
Park your surfboard by the door
There's no room up here
for such subjective realities
nor for the sirens wailing either
in Vaughan Williams' Antarctica
That is not what I meant at all at all
We're watching ocean waves during the eclipse
'live' on TV!
(Shadows of shadows on the walls of the Cave)

In the doom the women come and go
Heaps of this and that on gallery floors
(Mother snores)
So call it art and tell me if I'm dreaming
and just what *is* its double meaning
and when will it cohere?
But that's just the point my dear
Rome wasn't burnt in a day
We're falling through chaos to chaos
and we'll get there first this way
and laugh at you dancing your old dipsy-do
in your old Milky Way *mummy mia*

in your dear old figurative fantasia
of pointillist constellations
in picture-window landscapes
we all wished we lived in
as if we all hadn't all
read all the latest about
how we're all inside this
incoherent universe of broken symmetries
where all that falls
might fall *apart* in the end
into some kind of total darkness
although there once was a place perhaps
where *all* was light
which once was the place pray tell
some non-man-made god hung out

And so *tra-la tra-la*
It's *fin du siècle* again my dears
and the music of the spheres
some kind of mad mad laughter

THE PAINTER'S DREAM

I'm with Picasso and "Fernande in a Black Mantilla" looking tragic
    with turpentine like rain running down her shoulder
And I'm in Pontoise with Pissarro
And with Gauguin in "The Vanilla Grove"
And in the "Mountains of St. Remy" with Van Gogh
And at "The Bend in the Road through the Forest" with Cézanne
And with Vuillard in "The Place Vintimille"
And with Picasso and "El Loco" and his blue acrobats
And with Picasso shaking his fist at the sky in "Guernica"
And I'm Durer's Steeple-jack seen by Marianne Moore
And those harpies "The Demoiselles of Avignon" are glaring at me
    personally
And Degas' ballet dancers are dancing for Matisse and Monet and
    Renoir and all the Sunday painters of Paris and John Sloane and all
    the Sunday painters of America and most of the painters of the
    Hudson River School floating along so calm and holding hands with
    most of the West Coast Figurative painters and their Have a Nice
    Day cohorts
But I'm also with Malevich in his "Red Square" in the Beautiful Corner
And with Delacroix' "Liberty Leading the Masses"
And with Goya's groaning masses in "The Disasters of War"
And I'm rocking across the Atlantic with "Whistler's Mother"
And I'm crossing the Delaware with Washington standing in the boat
    against Navy regulations
And I'm with Bierstadt crossing the Rockies on a mule
And with Motherwell and DeKooning and Kline and Pollock and Larry
    Rivers in the broken light in the shaken light of the late late
    late twentieth century
And then I'm walking through a huge exhibition in the Whole World
    Museum of Art containing all the greatest paintings of the entire
    fine arts tradition of all the centuries of western civilization
When suddenly a wild-haired band bursts into the Museum and starts
    spraying paint-solvent onto all the paintings
And all the paint in all the paintings starts to run down onto the floors of

all the galleries forming fantastic new and exciting images of the end
of our little universe
And elite curators in Gucci shoes rush in and cut up the painted floors
and hang them on the walls while picturesque bohemian painters in
berets stagger through the halls *weeping*

"A HEAP OF BROKEN IMAGES"

Empty house on a horizon
         Two faces at a window
                  heads turned
    Barking dog on a leash extended
          Penis hung on a wall about to fall
  A hand raised
     with six fingers crossed
  A ladder leaning on the sky upended
A sea wave about to break upon a beach
  A bird about to cry in flight
Two mermaids singing each to each
         mark the place where a story ended
  A setting sun
    holds off the night
All of this in time suspended
    The universe holding its breath
There is a hush in the air
          Life pulses everywhere
There is no such thing as death

BAJA BEATITUDES

#1

The great gray *gaviota*
                and the two white gulls
     and the two old fishermen
                    ancient of days
       grizzled brothers grown to old age
               on this far beach
        hermanos in soledad
          the older of the two
              bent and bearded
        singing to the gulls
           in a high crazy voice
       talking childish to them
         as they float about
    on the calm surface
    in the first dawn
       in the early early morn
The younger brother
      stands silent in the door
           of their thatched hut
      their
         patched palm *palapa*
It is the older brother
     who sings and dances
         in his mind
 It is only he who crazily sings
       and laughs and chatters
    to the two white *gaviotas*
       that float about
   on the dawn waters
      waiting to be fed
He throws them scraps of bait
   and the gray *gaviota*
      swoops in upon them

              folding his painted wings
                        as he settles to the surface
          next to the old wood boat
          and the fisherman bent over
                    like a hunchback
                              or an ancient Greek god
              passing himself off
                              as a fisherman

It is Odysseus
                    in his old wandered age
          cast up
                    by the Sea of Cortez
                        (the sea routes squandered)
Or he is the other in the doorway
                        with his blind eye
                              looking out
The greedy gray *gaviota*
                        grabs the floating food
              and makes off
But now the fisherman
                        bails his boat
                              still chattering
          and pushes off in his boat
                        puts off in it
          forth upon the flat sea
                        bailing and rowing
It is he who still sings and laughs
                    and talks to the loud birds
          as he goes
                    They answer
                              with comical cawing
              almost like laughter mocking
And the fisherman mimics them
                        with the same crazy cawing
          as he rows away and away
                              into silence
          and grows smaller and smaller

22

                    and disappears at last
          over the horizon
                    to set his nets and buoys
                              in the deep deep waters
          of the Bahia de Concepcion
While his purblind brother
                    dumb with the dawn
                    of a million mornings
     stands mute upon the strand
                    in his own beatitude
          staring out
                    into the very heart
                    of silence
          over the becalmed waters
          below the very distant
                              Magritte mountains

As still another day prepares
                    for heat and solitude

                         #2

A t night the stars
          in their dark courses
                    breaded with light
     above the sumi-ink sea
wheel about
     on their immense
                    invisible wheel
perhaps myriad creatures caught
                    in unseen gill-nets
     or stretched upon a turning stage
     of some self-effacing
                    master dramatist
or they are no doubt
     all jewels within
                    some timeless turning clock
     that needs no winding

                    powered by
                              great god sun
They turn and turn
                    upon us
                              who gaze and gape
                    into the dense dark
                              stick figures
                                    in the world's end
              Giacometti walkers
                         two-faced Picassos
                                    (one face averted
                                         one straight up)
              seen at a
                         very great distance
Only here
              all is Aztec
                    all *indio*
              Toltec and Quetzal
              Cortezians not Cartesians
And in the dark dawn
                    in first light
                         the sea not sumi
                         but Aztec ochre
                         streaked with cactus green
              The ochre sea
                    the gold sea shimmers
                              with the dawn wind
                    which streaks the sea
                              rippling the gold cloth
              whereon a fisherman
                    raises his antique voice
                    in an antic Aztec call
                              to the great god of light
              who raises now
                         his huge radiant head
                              in golden helmet
                    over the rim of the world

Ah the ochre sea
              rustles with the sound of wind
                     (as in a field of dry corn)
And the far off fisherman
                    cries and cries again
      as his rope-bound rock anchor
                         sinks
          upon the transplanted ghosts
                         of Cortez' scuttled boats

#3

The polyglot sea
             ah the polyglot sea . . .
   sybils' syllables   fellaheen dialects
          all run together
     everywhere re-echoing . . .
         The wild wave
            the broken waters
     chittering waters of . . .
      rivering waters of . . .
       hither-and-thithering waters of . . .
battering the shores
               the far islands . . .
        Isolated languages
           stand up to it
              for a moment only
      or a century

Again
      again
        the talking wind
             slides its rough tongue
     over the coursing tides
        over the continents
           the flooded alluvias
     lashing the breakwaters

                    the broken battlements
            the jagged reefs
                    with its salty tongue
        coalescing all
                into one huge
                        polyphonic
                    liquid language
            babbled together
                            cobbled together
        into one polyphoboistrous
                running sea of speech
    Upon which mute ships race
                    toward a common humanity

BAJA REVISITED

Baja wild baja
still a last frontier
here on the left side of the world
still nothing but sand sand sand
deserts and mountains and wild ocean
cactii gesturing against the sky
by the Sea of Cortez
the highway an Aztec arrow
sun beating down
sky like sand
over the forsaken landscape
littered with wreckage
of a million jalopies
ghost trucks rusted out
twisted into faunas
of sand and rock
oxidized into oblivion
the drivers long ago run off
the coal-eyed *indios*
beaten by Spanish
English
French
Cortez and Guzman
followed by
Jesuits and Dominicans
stray gringos
poachers and outcasts
outlaws and desert rats
(up to no good)

And now the huge motor homes
sprouting CB radios and TVs
all rolling South
full of old white couples
seeking their last sun
hull down in Winnebagos

A REPORT ON A HAPPENING IN
WASHINGTON SQUARE SAN FRANCISCO

When the lovely bride and groom came out onto the grand front steps of the Catholic church of Saint Peter & Paul at 4:32 in the afternoon a knot of natives was waiting at the bottom of the steps including a bunch of bridesmaids and family friends all of whom were holding onto the straight strings of bright green balloons which were the exact same green as the bridesmaids' dresses And the bride was holding onto a pure white balloon which was naturally the same as her wedding gown and the groom was holding a black balloon that matched his black tail coat And the newlyweds proceeded to knot the strings of their two balloons together and then with a kind of whoop let them soar away while at the same instant all the people holding green balloons let theirs go with a little cheer And the beatific bride and her handsome groom laughed and waved as they descended toward the others with never a look up at the balloons that were zooming straight up into the blue sky and becoming smaller and smaller every instant while the newlyweds gaily climbed onto the waiting imitation San Francisco Cable Car upon which the bridesmaids were already perched and nobody casting even a glance at the flying balloons that now seemed to be heading South over downtown San Francisco with the black and white balloons keeping close together on their tether while the green balloons started spreading out all over And the groom and bride took their special seats at the front of the cable car which wasn't a real cable car at all since it had rubber wheels not attached to any cable which would have restricted its destiny And the happy couple were still waving and laughing and kissing each other and then ringing and ringing the cable car bell while the balloons that nobody looked at were now at least a couple of miles high in the distant sky that now seemed to be growing darker and darker with huge banks of cirrus clouds to the West toward which the tiny balloons now turned like a flock of birds winging seaward with two of them still close together while the others strung out further and further so that they began to look like lost sheep in an alpine landscape of towering white mountains While the cable car of a sudden started up with a great clanging of its bell as everyone cheered and waved without ever a look at the disappearing balloons of their lives so far away now that they looked like very distant mountain climbers scaling the walls of great glaciers in the final working out of their separate fates except for the two climbers still roped together As the cable car zoomed off westward on Filbert Street and on toward Russian Hill over which in farthest sky still could be seen the tiny black dots of the climbers going higher and higher and disappearing into their destinies in which even the two roped together would in the normal course of life lose their breath and shrivel away and fall to earth out of air

I GENITORI PERDUTI

The dove-white gulls
on the wet lawn in Washington Square
in the early morning fog
each a little ghost in the gloaming
Souls transmigrated maybe
from Hudson's shrouded shores
across all the silent years—
Which one's my maybe mafioso father
in his so white suit and black shoes
in his real estate office Forty-second Street
or at the front table wherever he went—
Which my dear lost mother with faded smile
locked away from me in time—
Which my big brother Charley
selling switching-signals all his life
on the New York Central—
And which good guy brother Clem
sweating in Sing Sing's darkest offices
deputy-warden thirty years
watching executions in the wooden armchair
(with leather straps and black hood)
He too gone mad with it in the end—
And which my nearest brother Harry
still kindest and dearest in a far suburb—
I see them now all turn to me at last
gull-eyed in the white dawn
about to call to me
across the silent grass

QUEENS CEMETERY, SETTING SUN

Airport bus from JFK
cruising through Queens
passing huge endless cemetery
by Long Island's old expressway
(once a dirt path for wheelless Indians)
myriad small tombstones tilted up
gesturing statues on parapets
stone arms or wings upraised
lost among illegible inscriptions
And the setting yellow sun
painting all of them
on one side only
with an ochre brush
Rows and rows and rows and rows
of small stone slabs
tilted toward the sun forever
While on the far horizon
Mannahatta's great stone slabs
skyscraper tombs and parapets
casting their own long black shadows
over all these long-haired graves
the final restless places
of old-country potato farmers
dustbin pawnbrokers
dead dagos and Dublin bouncers
tinsmiths and blacksmiths and roofers
house painters and house carpenters
cabinet makers and cigar makers
garment workers and streetcar motormen
railroad switchmen and signal salesmen
swabbers and sweepers and swampers
steam-fitters and key-punch operators
ward heelers and labor organizers
railroad dicks and smalltime mafiosi
shopkeepers and saloon keepers and doormen

icemen and middlemen and conmen
housekeepers and housewives and dowagers
French housemaids and Swedish cooks
Brooklyn barmaids and Bronxville butlers
opera singers and gandy dancers
pitchers and catchers
in the days of ragtime baseball
poolroom hustlers and fight promoters
Catholic sisters of charity
parish priests and Irish cops
Viennese doctors of delirium
now all abandoned in eternity
parcels in a dead-letter office
inscrutable addresses on them
beyond further deliverance
in an America wheeling past them
and disappearing oblivious
into East River's echoing tunnels
down the great American drain

SHERMAN'S MARCH REGLITTERIZED

Recently regilded
General Sherman marches bravely
through Central Park South
into Grand Army Plaza
led by a Delacroix lady liberty
(obviously pressed into service
by the military)
with slightly over-sized arm upraised
and carrying an extra-large olive branch
in her left hand
while from her back sprout
huge gelt wings
The General himself with cape thrown back
on this huge gold stallion
while on the grey stone ground
next to the horse's huge left leg
lies a torn branch
of some great old evergreen
as if in this wood
the General did behold
the much-touted
Golden Bough of antiquity
but had indeed discarded it
having greater money-trees in mind
as he charged forward
on this noble stallion
longing to be Pegasus
And now both the General and his lady
looking so content
to have been recently reglitterized
and striding straight on into
the traffic at 59th & Fifth—
And will they be turned back
at the Plaza Hotel
like so many other outlanders before them

or will they perhaps continue on
to make the world safer for capitalism
and actually take off
on those great gelt wings
zooming straight on downtown to
their own rock-solid broker
in grand old Wall Street itself
whose many walls still stand
in the very gelty pumping heart
of the beast?

THE CANTICLE OF JACK KEROUAC

1.

F<small>ar</small> from the sea far from the sea
>   of Breton fishermen
>   the white clouds scudding
>   over Lowell
>   and the white birches the
>   bare white birches
>   along the blear night roads
>   flashing by in darkness
>   (where once he rode
>   in Pop's old Plymouth)
> And the birch-white face
>   of a Merrimac madonna
>   shadowed in streetlight
>   by Merrimac's shroudy waters
>   —a leaf blown
>   upon sea wind
>   out of Brittany
>   over endless oceans

2.

T<small>here</small> is a garden in the memory of America
There is a nightbird in its memory
There is an *andante cantabile*
in a garden in the memory
of America
In a secret garden
in a private place
a song a melody
a nightsong echoing
in the memory of America
In the sound of a nightbird
outside a Lowell window

In the cry of kids
in tenement yards at night
In the deep sound
of a woman murmuring
a woman singing broken melody
in a shuttered room
in an old wood house
in Lowell
As the world cracks by
                         thundering
like a lost lumber truck
                    on a steep grade
          in Kerouac America
The woman sits silent now
                    rocking backward
       to Whistler's Mother in Lowell
             and all the tough old
                         Canuck mothers
                 and Jack's Mémère
And they continue rocking
    And may still on stormy nights show through
          as a phantom after-image
                    on silent TV screens
             a flickered after-image
                    that will not go away
          in Moody Street
             in Beaulieu Street
                in 'dirtstreet Sarah Avenue'
    in Pawtucketville
    And in the Church of St. Jean Baptiste

                    3.

And the Old Worthen Bar
                    in Lowell Mass. at midnight
       in the now of Nineteen Eighty-seven
Kerouackian revellers
                    crowd the wood booths

                    ancient with carved initials
                         of a million drinking bouts
                         the clouts of the
                                   Shrouded Stranger
                    upon each wood pew
          where the likes of Kerouack lumberjack
                    feinted their defiance
                              of dung and death
Ah the broken wood and the punka fans still turning
          (pull-cord wavings
                              of the breath of the Buddha)
          still lost in Lowell's
                              'vast tragedies of darkness'
                    with Jack

                              4.

And the Four Sisters Diner
          also known as 'The Owl'
Sunday morning now
                    March Eighty-seven
or any year of Sunday specials
Scrambled eggs and chopped ham
 the bright booths loaded with families
          Lowell Greek and Gaspé French
                    Joual patois and Argos argot
          Spartan slaves escaped
                         into the New World
               here incarnate
                         in rush of blood of
                         American Sunday morning
And "Ti-Jean" Jack Kerouac
     comes smiling in
                    baseball cap cocked up
               hungry for mass
                         in this Church of All Hungry Saints
               haunt of all-night Owls
                              blessing every booth . . .

5.

Ah he the Silent Smiler
  the one
           with the lumberjack shirt
      and cap with flaps askew
              blowing his hands in winter
         as if to light a flame
The Shrouded Stranger knew him
    as Ti-Jean the Smiler
        grooking past redbrick mill buildings
        down by the riverrun
                   (O mighty Merrimac
                          'thunderous husher')
          where once upon a midnight then
        young Ti-Jean danced with Mémère
            in the moondrowned light
And rolled upon the greensward
    his mother and lover
      all one with Buddha
           in his arms

6.

And then Ti-Jean Jack with Joual tongue
    disguised as an American fullback in plaid shirt
      crossing and recrossing America
                 in speedy cars
    a Dr. Sax's shadow shadowing him
   like a shroudy cloud over the landscape
    Song of the Open Road sung drunken
        with Whitman and Jack London and Thomas Wolfe
      still echoing through
               a Nineteen Thirties America
               A Nineteen Forties America
               an America now long gone
        except in broken down dusty old
                   Greyhound Bus stations

in small lost towns
Ti-Jean's vision of America
seen from a moving car window
the same as Wolfe's lonely
sweeping vision
glimpsed from a coach-train long ago
('And thus did he see first the dark land')
And so Jack
in an angel midnight bar
somewhere West of Middle America
where one drunk madonna
(shades of one on a Merrimac corner)
makes him a gesture with her eyes
a blue gesture
and Ti-Jean answers
only with his eyes
And the night goes on with them
And the light comes up on them
making love in a parking lot

7.

In the dark of his fellaheen night
in the light of the illuminated
Stations of the Cross
and the illuminated Grotto
down behind the Funeral Home
by roar of river
where now Ti-Jean alone
(returned to Lowell
in one more doomed
Wolfian attempt
to Go Home Again)
gropes past the Twelve Stations of the Cross
reciting aloud the French inscriptions
in his Joual accent
which makes the plaster French Christ
laugh and cry

as He hefts His huge Cross
up the Eternal Hill
And a very real tear drops
in the Grotto
from the face
of the stoned Virgin

8.

Light upon light
The Mountain
keeps still

9.

Hands over ears
He steals away
with the Bell. . . .

*Writ in Lowell and Conway and Boston Mass. and San Francisco
March–April 1987*

SPIRIT OF THE CRUSADES

Stoney Wales
with its slate-grey roofs
in slate-grey Cardiff
and its greystone houses on greystone terraces
and its great high statue of
"The Spirit of the Crusades"
in the Wales National Museum
portraying a medieval knight
in grey metal armor and helmet
with visor down
on a great grey steed
with four grey foot soldiers
in close march about him
(two at the head of the horse
two behind)
wearing World War One helmets
and carrying World War One rifles
with fixed bayonets
And the Crusades are over
but they are still marching
over the grey sea-locked land
in a dead march
straight through the twentieth century

BELATED PALINODE FOR
DYLAN THOMAS

In Wales at Laugharne at last I stand beside
  his cliff-perched writing shed
    above the coursing waters
      where the hawk hangs still
        above the cockle-strewn shingle
Where he walked in a glory of all his days
  (before the weather turned around)
And *aie! aie!* a waterbird far away
  cries and cries again
    over St. Johns Hill
And in his tilted boathouse now
  a tape of himself is playing—
    his lush voice
      his plush voice
        his posh accent
          (too BBC-fulsome, cried the Welsh)
          now echoes through his little
            upstairs room
And *aie! aie!*
  echo the waterbirds once again
Beyond his sounding shed
  a fig tree hides the sea
    A fishboat heeled over
      a grebe afloat far out
      a coracle abandoned
        a rusted coaler out of Cardiff still
        a bold green headland lost in sun
Beyond which lie (across an ocean and a continent)
  San Francisco's white wood houses
    and a poet's sun-bleached cottage
      on Bolinas' far lagoon
        with its wind-torn Little Mesa
          (so very like St. Johns Hill)

A single kestrel soars over
   riding the salt wind
     'high tide and the heron's call'
             still echoing
    (*Aie! aie!* it calls and calls again)
As in his listing boathouse now
   his great recorded voice runs out
     (grave as a gravedigger in his grave)
      leaving a sounding void of light
       for poets and herons to fill
(Drowned down in New York's White Horse Tavern
   he went not gentle into his good night)
And Far West poets calling still
   over St. Johns Hill
     to the loveliest poet of all our days
     sweet singer of Swansea
       lushed singer of Laugharne
       Dylan of all our days

"THE SEA IS CALM TONIGHT"

The sea is calm tonight
off Dover Beach
The birds at dusk
cry out syllables
of some deconstructed word
we are yet unable
to decipher
to explain existence
And they lift the last light
with their wings
And fly away with it
over the horizon
Keeping the secret

GOYA & THE SLEEP OF REASON

The dark stone statue of Goya
    stands between the trees
        at the side entrance of
            the Museo del Prado
He wears a long greatcoat
    and carries a tall beaver hat
Larger than life he
    strides forward purposely
  on a pedestal on top of
    a four-sided bas-relief
carved in white stone
    in which are depicted
        various struggling figures
    from his outrageous collection
        of humans and inhumans
  at the base of which is incised
      el sueño de la razón
        produce monstruos
A stone man sleeps or weeps
      right above the monsters
  with winged bats
    around him
The late morning sun
      glints off Goya
  and shadows of the leaves
      of the acacia trees
    fall on him
      as if the leaves themselves
      were falling
        (They do not)
I study his face
for some small sign of recognition
but his long hard look
      is directed beyond me

Reason sleeps beneath him
        but above
                against the sky's blue immensity
        all is intensely awake
                in the steady
                    and atrocious clarity
                        of his distant gaze

GROTTAMARE

Turquoise sea off Grottamare
Grottamare and its sea-caves echoing
                        beside the Adriatic
        Echo of siren song
                still reaches me
                        inside the silent train

                Once more the lost voices
                                calling undersea

        Ah but
                naturally
                        it is all illusion
        The fog lies heavily
                        in the olive trees
                Morning is made by the clock
                        and not by light
                                which only exists in our minds
                Men and women sleep
                        in their usual darkness
                Only the light
                        asleep in their eyes
                gives any hint
                        of an iridescent future
                                of an incandescent destiny
While far out
                beyond the far islands
        the sea sends back
                        its turquoise answer

ROMAN MORN

Ah these sweet Roman mornings—
　　I open the shutters
　　　　high above the back courtyard
　　and look out over the
　　　　　　　silent roofs . . .
　　　　the air still cool . . .
　　　　　　no birds on the tile chimneys . . .
　　　shutters still shut across the way . . .
　　　a windless weathervane far off . . .
　　　a whistle in the street below . . .
Now there's a pigeon
　　　　flutters a wing in an eave
　　　　on terracotta tilings
Ah now a white dove
　　　　alights on a cupola
　　as first sun slants through
The sun
　　floods over
　　　　　Shadows stretch out
　　　　　on rooftop gardens
There is a sweetness in the air
　　　The silent dove turns about
　　　　　on the bent tiles
They are opening the shutters
　　on the back side
　　　　of the Palazzo Farnese
　A phrase of French floats up
　　　　　　sounding alien
Somewhere a woman starts to sing
　　　　　a snatch of opera
Somewhere an angelus starts to ring
Somewhere a woman shouts *Angelo, Angelo!*
Somewhere he washes off his sins
The day begins and begins

TUNISIAN NOSTALGIA

B are white marble room
                in that white hotel
          on a high bluff
                over the sea
                          in Carthage
The huge French doors open
          on the too blue sea
     Flickered reflections of waves
                on the high ceiling
          over the big bed
               with the so-white muslin sheets
          and the white grey marble floors
                          cool to the bare feet
And through a door ajar
                    two bodies glimpsed
          on a bed in heat of noon
     an open bottle of retzina
                on the floor
And then the door swung shut
               the blinds drawn down
     And then the laughter and
          the kissing and
          the crying
               overheard
                    through the transom
     in that darkened room
                rented for a day long ago

THE CAT

The cat
    licks its paw and
lies down in
            the bookshelf nook
                            She
        can lie in a
            sphinx position
    without moving for so
                many hours
and then turn her head
            to me and
                rise and stretch
    and turn
        her back to me and
        lick her paw again as if
                no real time had passed
        It hasn't
            and she is the sphinx with
        all the time in the world
                in the desert of her time
        The cat
            knows where flies die
                sees ghosts in motes of air
                    and shadows in sunbeams
She hears
        the music of the spheres and
    the hum in the wires of houses
            and the hum of the universe
    in interstellar spaces
                            but
        prefers domestic places
            and the hum of the heater

SANDINISTA AVIONCITOS

The little airplanes of the heart
with their brave little propellers
What can they do
against the winds of darkness
even as butterflies are beaten back
by hurricanes
yet do not die
They lie in wait wherever
they can hide and hang
their fine wings folded
and when the killer-wind dies
they flutter forth again
into the new-blown light
live as leaves

DEFLOWERING

Life deflowers itself
petal by petal
One by one the leaves
fall away
like lovers from each other
Pistils and stamens
reveal themselves
to each other
And the seeds fall too
and all begins again
Ah what's to be done
with these leaves these seeds
still falling and falling
what to be done
with these fronds still falling
into the dark night of dying
where still stir
the still dumb birds
of our desiring
Even as now
under the dark trees
where the crickets are
suddenly she stops laughing
puts his hands
upon her breasts

LADAKH BUDDHESS BIKER

The Ladakh Buddhess is watching me
with her witchy eyes
on the corner of Columbus & Broadway
A gold button on her temple
between the eyes with the blue pupils
her eyes with blue eyebrows
not designed to blink
her eyelids like fenders
on old Oldsmobiles
her corneas red and blue
as if from loving & weeping too much
over our samsara
Eternally feminist
her headlight eyes beam at me
as if the sight of me
might make her finally
lower those heavy lids
I notice now she's seated on
a huge hog called Harley
her leather legs hugging its body
in a retro lotus position
Suddenly the traffic light changes
and she roars off still unblinking
through the late late traffic
of our Kali Yuga age

ASCENDING OVER OHIO

The angels coming down the aisles
have their wings on backwards
They are not wings for flying
but gossamer illusions
making these airline ladies
the ministers of my madness
even though each one wears
the same airline uniform
with a spare set of wings on lapels
each is also my ministering angel
my *belle dame sans merci*
come down to earth to fetch me
for the final flight to the heavens
where fly back and forth
the transworld spirits
of all the greatest gods
Buddha floats by holding the Christchild
in a Chinese scroll of sky
unrolling before us
as we ascend
over Warren Ohio
where fifty thousand lost bodies look up
as I release a shower of golden parachutes
with fifty thousand re-inflatable balloons
and fifty thousand valid passports
to the rest of the imaginary universe
where live and love and sing
the most ravenously beautiful bodies & souls
in all eternity
As one comes down the aisle now
spreading her gossamer wings
over me
and offering me
the sweet pneumatic ecstasy
of her airborne breasts

ONE OF THESE DAYS

When I am old
will they accept what I say
as the absolute truth
and call me *maestro*
and pin the cross of light on me
And if they do, oh if they do
will it have been worth it after all
all the broken sentences begun again
all the illusory triumphs
which could only happen on Sundays
when all the banks are closed
and the bankrupt churches open
and all the lotteries won
only to find the tickets printed
with evaporating ink
and the last horse in the last race
jumping the last fence to freedom
and I standing in the winner's circle
with a wreath around my neck
wondering which blond will kiss me
as the mariachi band plays
Happy Days Are Here Again
or The Battle Hymn of the Republic
and a parade goes by
to the distant plaza
where imbeciles wearing tinsel wings
drop from the trees?

SELECTED POEMS

AWAY ABOVE A HARBORFUL . . .

Away above a harborful
                        of caulkless houses
among the charley noble chimneypots
                of a rooftop rigged with clotheslines
        a woman pastes up sails
                        upon the wind
hanging out her morning sheets
                        with wooden pins
                O lovely mammal
                        her nearly naked breasts
            throw taut shadows
                        when she stretches up
to hang at last the last of her
                        so white washed sins
        but it is wetly amorous
                        and winds itself about her
            clinging to her skin
                        So caught with arms
                                        upraised
        she tosses back her head
                        in voiceless laughter
    and in choiceless gesture then
                        shakes out gold hair

while in the reachless seascape spaces

                between the blown white shrouds

    stand out the bright steamers

                        to kingdom come

JUST AS I USED TO SAY

Just as I used to say
                    love comes harder to the aged
because they've been running
                    on the same old rails too long
    and then when the sly switch comes along
                                    they miss the turn
        and burn up the wrong rail while
                        the gay caboose goes flying
            and the steamengine driver don't recognize
                            them new electric horns
and the aged run out on the rusty spur
                            which ends up in
                    the dead grass where
        the rusty tincans and bedsprings and old razor
                blades and moldy mattresses
                                    lie
        and the rail breaks off dead
                            right there
            though the ties go on awhile
                            and the aged
say to themselves
                Well
                    this must be the place
                we were supposed to lie down
And they do

                while the bright saloon careens along away
        on a high
                hilltop
                    its windows full of bluesky and lovers
                with flowers
                        their long hair streaming
                        and all of them laughing

and waving and
                    whispering to each other
and looking out and
                    wondering what that graveyard
    where the rails end
                    is

IN HINTERTIME PRAXITELES . . .

In hintertime Praxiteles
   laid about him with a golden maul
 striking into stone
     his alabaster ideals
uttering all
   the sculptor's lexicon
      in visible syllables
   He cast bronze trees
      petrified a chameleon on one
    made stone doves
      fly
    His calipers measured bridges
   and lovers
  and certain other superhumans whom
he caught upon their dusty way
      to death

   They never reached it then

      You still can almost see
    their breath
      Their stone eyes staring
  thru three thousand years
     allay our fears of aging

  although Praxiteles himself
      at twenty-eight lay dead

   for sculpture isn't for
      young men
  as Constantin Brancusi
     at a later hour
    said

IN PARIS IN A LOUD DARK WINTER

In Paris in a loud dark winter

        when the sun was something in Provence

when I came upon the poetry

        of René Char

    I saw Vaucluse again

        in a summer of sauterelles

  its fountains full of petals

        and its river thrown down

through all the burnt places

        of that almond world

and the fields full of silence

        though the crickets sang

  with their legs

        And in the poet's plangent dream I saw

no Lorelei upon the Rhone

        nor angels debarked at Marseilles

but couples going nude into the sad water

                                        in the profound lasciviousness of spring

      in an algebra of lyricism

                      which I am still deciphering

SAROLLA'S WOMEN IN THEIR
PICTURE HATS . . .

Sarolla's women in their picture hats
stretched upon his canvas beaches
                              beguiled the Spanish
                    Impressionists

                         And were they fraudulent pictures
of the world
           the way the light played on them
                                        creating illusions
        of love?

           I cannot help but think
                         that their 'reality'
was almost as real as
                 my memory of today

              when the last sun hung on the hills
              and I heard the day falling
              like the gulls that fell
              almost to land

           while the last picnickers lay and loved
                              in the blowing yellow broom
resisted and resisting
                 tearing themselves apart

                                        again

                                        again
        until the last hot hung climax
        which could at last no longer be resisted
                         made them moan
        And night's trees stood up

AND SHE 'LIKE A YOUNG YEAR . . .'

And she 'like a young year
walking thru the earth'
in the Bois de Boulogne that time
or as I remember her
stepping out of a bathtub
in that gold flat she had
corner of
Boulevard des Italiens

Oh they say she tried everything
before the end
took up television and crosswords
even crocheting
and things like that
and came to have the air
before the end
(as her favorite poet described her)
of 'always carrying flowers
toward some far
abandoned tomb'

which doesn't surprise me now
that I come to think of it

The struck seed was in her

IT WAS A FACE WHICH DARKNESS
COULD KILL . . .

It was a face which darkness could kill
in an instant
a face as easily hurt
by laughter or light

'We *think* differently at night'
she told me once
lying back languidly

And she would quote Cocteau

'I feel there is an angel in me' she'd say
'whom I am constantly
shocking'

Then she would smile and look away
light a cigarette for me
sigh and rise
and stretch
her sweet anatomy

let fall a stocking

LONDON CROSSFIGURED

London

crossfigured
creeping with trams

and the artists on sundays
in the summer
all 'tracking Nature'
in the suburbs

It
could have been anyplace
but it wasn't
It was
London

and when someone shouted over

that they had got a model

I ran out across the court

but then
when the model started taking off
her clothes
there was nothing underneath
I mean to say
she took off her shoes
and found no feet
took off her top
and found no tit
under it
and I must say she did look
a bit
ASTOUNDED

                    just standing there
                        looking down
                    at where her legs were
                                        not

        But so very carefully then   .
                                    she put her clothes back on
and as soon as she was dressed again
                                    completely
                    she was completely
                                    all right

            Do it again! cried someone
                                    rushing for his easel

        But she was afraid to

                            and gave up modelling

    and forever after

                        slept in her clothes

WITH BELLS FOR HOOVES IN
SOUNDING STREETS . . .

With bells for hooves in sounding streets

that terrible horse the unicorn

came on

and cropped a medlar from a tree
and where he dropped the seed
sprang up a virgin

oh she sprang up upon his back
and rode off tittering to a stair
where pieces of string lay scattered
everywhere

Now when she saw the string so white
so lovely and so beautiful
and looking like
Innocence itself
she got down and reached for a nice
straight piece

but it had a head
and it bit
her beautiful place
So (she said)

this is how it all began

Next time I'll know

But it was too late and they buried her

THAT FELLOW ON THE BOATTRAIN
WHO INSISTED . . .

That fellow on the boattrain who insisted
on playing blackjack
had teeth that stuck out
like lighthouses on a rocky coast

but
he had no eyes to see
the dusk flash past

horses in orchards
noiselessly running
bunches of birds
thrown up

and the butterflies of yesterday
that flittered on
my mind

HEAVEN . . .

Heaven
            was only half as far that night

at the poetry recital

            listening to the burnt phrases

when I heard the poet have

                        a rhyming erection

then look away with a

                        lost look

'Every animal' he said at last

'After intercourse is sad'

But the back-row lovers
                        looked oblivious

            and glad

THE WORLD IS A BEAUTIFUL
PLACE . . .

The world is a beautiful place
                      to be born into
if you don't mind happiness
                not always being
                            so very much fun
    if you don't mind a touch of hell
                    now and then
        just when everything is fine
                because even in heaven
           they don't sing
              all the time

The world is a beautiful place
                    to be born into
if you don't mind some people dying
                    all the time
       or maybe only starving
                  some of the time
     which isn't half so bad
              if it isn't you

Oh the world is a beautiful place
                    to be born into
    if you don't much mind
           a few dead minds
     in the higher places
            or a bomb or two
       now and then
            in your upturned faces
or such other improprieties
            as our Name Brand society
      is prey to
          with its men of distinction
   and its men of extinction

                                        and its priests
                        and other patrolmen

                                                and its various segregations
                    and congressional investigations
                                        and other constipations
                        that our fool flesh
                                is heir to

    Yes the world is the best place of all
                                for a lot of such things as
                    making the fun scene
                                and making the love scene
    and making the sad scene
                    and singing low songs and having inspirations
                    and walking around
                                looking at everything
                                        and smelling flowers
                    and goosing statues
                                and even thinking
                                        and kissing people and
                    making babies and wearing pants
                                                and waving hats and
                                dancing
                        and going swimming in rivers
                                on picnics
                                in the middle of the summer
                    and just generally
                                'living it up'
    Yes
        but then right in the middle of it
                                comes the smiling

                        mortician

READING YEATS I DO NOT THINK . . .

Reading Yeats I do not think
of Ireland
but of midsummer New York
and of myself back then
reading that copy I found
on the Thirdavenue El

the El
with its flyhung fans
and its signs reading
SPITTING IS FORBIDDEN

the El
careening thru its thirdstory world
with its thirdstory people
in their thirdstory doors
looking as if they had never heard
of the ground

an old dame
watering her plant
or a joker in a straw
putting a stickpin in his peppermint tie
and looking just like he had nowhere to go
but coneyisland

or an undershirted guy
rocking in his rocker
watching the El pass by
as if he expected it to be different
each time

Reading Yeats I do not think
of Arcady

and of its woods which Yeats thought dead
                                        I think instead
        of all the gone faces
                        getting off at midtown places
        with their hats and their jobs
        and of that lost book I had
                        with its blue cover and its white inside
where a pencilhand had written
                                HORSEMAN, PASS BY!

SWEET AND VARIOUS THE WOODLARK . . .

Sweet and various the woodlark

who sings at the unbought gate

and yet how many

wild beasts
how many mad
in the civil thickets

Hölderlin
in his stone tower
or in that kind carpenter's house
at Tübingen

or then Rimbaud
his 'nightmare and logic'
a sophism of madness

But we have our own more recent
who also fatally assumed
that some direct connection
does exist between
language and reality
word and world

which is a laugh
if you ask me

I too have drunk and seen
the spider

IN GOYA'S GREATEST SCENES WE SEEM TO SEE . . .

In Goya's greatest scenes we seem to see
                              the people of the world
            exactly at the moment when
                  they first attained the title of
                                          'suffering humanity'
            They writhe upon the page
                              in a veritable rage
                                          of adversity
            Heaped up
                  groaning with babies and bayonets
                                          under cement skies
            in an abstract landscape of blasted trees
                  bent statues bats wings and beaks
                              slippery gibbets
                  cadavers and carnivorous cocks
            and all the final hollering monsters
                  of the
                              'imagination of disaster'
            they are so bloody real
                              it is as if they really still existed

      And they do

            Only the landscape is changed

      They still are ranged along the roads
            plagued by legionnaires
                  false windmills and demented roosters

They are the same people
                                only further from home
            on freeways fifty lanes wide
                        on a concrete continent
                                spaced with bland billboards
                        illustrating imbecile illusions of happiness

            The scene shows fewer tumbrils
                                but more strung-out citizens
                                        in painted cars
                        and they have strange license plates
                        and engines
                                that devour America

SAILING THRU THE STRAITS OF DEMOS

Sailing thru the straits of Demos
    we saw symbolic birds
                shrieking over us
      while eager eagles hovered
            and elephants in bathtubs
   floated past us out to sea
               strumming bent mandolins
  and bailing for old glory with their ears
             while patriotic maidens
    wearing paper poppies
          and eating bonbons
    ran along the shores
          wailing after us
and while we lashed ourselves to masts
          and stopt our ears with chewing gum
   dying donkeys on high hills
        sang low songs
    and gay cows flew away
          chanting Athenian anthems
  as their pods turned to tulips
         and heliocopters from Helios
     flew over us
        dropping free railway tickets
   from Lost Angeles to Heaven
         and promising Free Elections
    So that
      we set up mast and sail
on that swart ship once more
       and so set forth once more
   forth upon the gobbly sea
       loaded with liberated vestal virgins
and discus throwers reading *Walden*
    but
     shortly after reaching

                    the strange suburban shores
        of that great American
                    demi-democracy
        looked at each other
                        with a mild surprise
            silent upon a peak
                        in Darien

THE POET'S EYE OBSCENELY
SEEING . . .

The poet's eye obscenely seeing

sees the surface of the round world

> with its drunk rooftops
>
> and wooden oiseaux on clotheslines
>
> and its clay males and females
>
> with hot legs and rosebud breasts
>
> in rollaway beds

and its trees full of mysteries

and its Sunday parks and speechless statues

and its America

> with its ghost towns and empty Ellis Islands

and its surrealist landscape of

> > mindless prairies
> >
> > supermarket suburbs
> >
> > steamheated cemeteries
> >
> > and protesting cathedrals

a kissproof world of plastic toiletseats tampax and taxis

> drugged store cowboys and las vegas virgins
>
> disowned indians and cinemad matrons
>
> unroman senators and conscientious non-objectors

and all the other fatal shorn-up fragments

of the immigrant's dream come too true

and mislaid

among the sunbathers

SOMETIME DURING ETERNITY . . .

Sometime during eternity
                         some guys show up
and one of them
               who shows up real late
                              is a kind of carpenter
          from some square-type place
                              like Galilee
          and he starts wailing
                         and claiming he is hip
          to who made heaven
                              and earth
                              and that the cat
          who really laid it on us
                              is his Dad

          And moreover
            he adds
                    It's all writ down
                              on some scroll-type parchments
          which some henchmen
               leave lying around the Dead Sea somewheres
               a long time ago
                         and which you won't even find
          for a coupla thousand years or so
                              or at least for
     nineteen hundred and fortyseven
                              of them
                    to be exact
                         and even then
          nobody really believes them
                              or me
                              for that matter
          You're hot
                    they tell him

And they cool him

They stretch him on the Tree to cool

    And everybody after that
                    is always making models
        of this Tree
            with Him hung up
and always crooning His name
        and calling Him to come down
      and sit in
          on their combo
    as if he is *the* king cat
            who's got to blow
  or they can't quite make it

    Only he don't come down
           from His Tree

Him just hang there
        on His Tree
looking real Petered out
      and real cool
           and also
    according to a roundup
        of late world news
from the usual unreliable sources
           real dead

THEY WERE PUTTING UP THE STATUE . . .

They were putting up the statue
of Saint Francis
in front of the church
of Saint Francis
in the city of San Francisco
in a little side street
just off the Avenue
where no birds sang
and the sun was coming up on time
in its usual fashion
and just beginning to shine
on the statue of Saint Francis
where no birds sang

And a lot of old Italians
were standing all around
in the little side street
just off the Avenue
watching the wily workers
who were hoisting up the statue
with a chain and a crane
and other implements
And a lot of young reporters
in button-down clothes
were taking down the words
of one young priest
who was propping up the statue
with all his arguments

And all the while
while no birds sang
any Saint Francis Passion
and while the lookers kept looking
up at Saint Francis

with his arms outstretched
                                    to the birds which weren't there
a very tall and very purely naked
                                                            young virgin
    with very long and very straight
                                            straw hair
    and wearing only a very small
                                                    bird's nest
        in a very existential place
                                            kept passing thru the crowd
                                                    all the while
            and up and down the steps
                                        in front of Saint Francis
        her eyes downcast all the while
                                                and singing to herself

WHAT COULD SHE SAY TO THE
FANTASTIC FOOLYBEAR . . .

What could she say to the fantastic foolybear
and what could she say to brother
and what could she say
                         to the cat with future feet
and what could she say to mother
after that time that she lay lush
                              among the lolly flowers
        on that hot riverbank
              where ferns fell away in the broken air
                    of the breath of her lover
    and birds went mad
                        and threw themselves from trees
to taste still hot upon the ground
                        the spilled sperm seed

IN GOLDEN GATE PARK THAT DAY . . .

In Golden Gate Park that day
               a man and his wife were coming along
    thru the enormous meadow
           which was the meadow of the world
He was wearing green suspenders
            and carrying an old beat-up flute
                 in one hand
    while his wife had a bunch of grapes
           which she kept handing out
                   individually
              to various squirrels
                as if each
              were a little joke

    And then the two of them came on
               thru the enormous meadow
which was the meadow of the world
           and then
      at a very still spot where the trees dreamed
     and seemed to have been waiting thru all time
               for them
      they sat down together on the grass
          without looking at each other
    and ate oranges
        without looking at each other
          and put the peels
     in a basket which they seemed
         to have brought for that purpose
     without looking at each other

And then
     he took his shirt and undershirt off
   but kept his hat on
         sideways

                              and without saying anything
          fell asleep under it
                              And his wife just sat there looking
at the birds which flew about
  calling to each other
                    in the stilly air
        as if they were questioning existence
                or trying to recall something forgotten

But then finally
                she too lay down flat
                                    and just lay there looking up
                                            at nothing
            yet fingering the old flute
                                which nobody played
            and finally looking over
                    at him
      without any particular expression
                                except a certain awful look
            of terrible depression

SEE IT WAS LIKE THIS WHEN . . .

S_{ee}
  it was like this when
              we waltz into this place
a couple of Papish cats
              is doing an Aztec two-step
And I says
          Dad let's cut
but then this dame
              comes up behind me see
                  and says
              You and me could really exist
Wow I says
          Only the next day
          she has bad teeth
              and really hates
                          poetry

DON'T LET THAT HORSE . . .

Don't let that horse
                    eat that violin

    cried Chagall's mother

                        But he
                kept right on
                        painting

And became famous

And kept on painting
                    The Horse With Violin In Mouth

And when he finally finished it
he jumped up upon the horse
                            and rode away
            waving the violin

And then with a low bow gave it
to the first naked nude he ran across

And there were no strings
                        attached

I HAVE NOT LAIN WITH BEAUTY
ALL MY LIFE . . .

I have not lain with beauty all my life
              telling over to myself
                                    its most rife charms

    I have not lain with beauty all my life
                                    and lied with it as well
              telling over to myself
                        how beauty never dies
          but lies apart
                        among the aborigines
                                          of art
                  and far above the battlefields
                                          of love

      It is above all that
                      oh yes
      It sits upon the choicest of
                        Church seats
  up there where art directors meet
  to choose the things for immortality

                        And they have lain with beauty
                all their lives
                        And they have fed on honeydew
          and drunk the wines of Paradise
                        so that they know exactly how
          a thing of beauty is a joy
              forever and forever
                        and how it never never
                  quite can fade
                        into a money-losing nothingness
          Oh no I have not lain
                        on Beauty Rests like this

                    afraid to rise at night
                            for fear that I might somehow miss
            some movement beauty might have made
                Yet I have slept with beauty
                                        in my own weird way
            and I have made a hungry scene or two
                                    with beauty in my bed
        and so spilled out another poem or two
            and so spilled out another poem or two
                                upon the Bosch-like world

CONSTANTLY RISKING
ABSURDITY . . .

Constantly risking absurdity
                        and death
            whenever he performs
                        above the heads
                                of his audience
        the poet like an acrobat
                        climbs on rime
                                to a high wire of his own making
    and balancing on eyebeams
                        above a sea of faces
            paces his way
                        to the other side of day
        performing entrechats
                        and sleight-of-foot tricks
    and other high theatrics
                        and all without mistaking
                any thing
                        for what it may not be

        For he's the super realist
                        who must perforce perceive
                taut truth
                        before the taking of each stance or step
    in his supposed advance
                        toward that still higher perch
    where Beauty stands and waits
                        with gravity
        to start her death-defying leap
    And he
        a little charleychaplin man
                        who may or may not catch
        her fair eternal form
                        spreadeagled in the empty air
            of existence

IN WOODS WHERE MANY RIVERS RUN

In woods where many rivers run
                    among the unbent hills
    and fields of our childhood
                    where ricks and rainbows mix in memory
although our 'fields' were streets
                    I see again those myriad mornings rise
    when every living thing
                    cast its shadow in eternity
    and all day long the light
                    like early morning
        with its sharp shadows shadowing
                    a paradise
        that I had hardly dreamed of
                    nor hardly knew to think
        of this unshaved today
                    with its derisive rooks
    that rise above dry trees
                    and caw and cry
and question every other
                    spring and thing

THE PENNYCANDYSTORE BEYOND
THE EL . . .

The pennycandystore beyond the El
is where I first
                fell in love
                        with unreality
Jellybeans glowed in the semi-gloom
of that september afternoon
A cat upon the counter moved among
                        the licorice sticks
            and tootsie rolls
        and Oh Boy Gum

Outside the leaves were falling as they died

A wind had blown away the sun

A girl ran in
Her hair was rainy
Her breasts were breathless in the little room

Outside the leaves were falling
                    and they cried
                        Too soon! too soon!

WE SQUAT UPON THE BEACH OF LOVE

We squat upon the beach of love
 among Picasso mandolins struck full of sand
   and buried catspaws that know no sphinx
   and picnic papers
    dead crabs' claws
    and starfish prints

We squat upon the beach of love
 among the beached mermaids
   with their bawling babies and bald husbands
   and homemade wooden animals
    with icecream spoons for feet
     which cannot walk or love
      except to eat

We squat upon the brink of love
 and are secure as only squatters are
  among the puddled leavings
      of salt sex's tides
  and the sweet semen rivulets
     and limp buried peckers
 in the sand's soft flesh

And still we laugh
 and still we run
  and still we throw ourselves
    upon love's boats
   but it is deeper
     and much later
      than we think
   and all goes down
    and all out lovebuoys fail us

And we drink and drown

DOVE STA AMORE . . .

Dove sta amore
Where lies love
Dove sta amore
Here lies love
The ring dove love
In lyrical delight
Hear love's hillsong
Love's true willsong
Love's low plainsong
Too sweet painsong
In passages of night
Dove sta amore
Here lies love
The ring dove love
Dove sta amore
Here lies love

I AM WAITING

I am waiting for my case to come up
and I am waiting
for a rebirth of wonder
and I am waiting for someone
to really discover America
and wail
and I am waiting
for the discovery
of a new symbolic western frontier
and I am waiting
for the American Eagle
to really spread its wings
and straighten up and fly right
and I am waiting
for the Age of Anxiety
to drop dead
and I am waiting
for the war to be fought
which will make the world safe
for anarchy
and I am waiting
for the final withering away
of all governments
and I am perpetually awaiting
a rebirth of wonder

I am waiting for the Second Coming
and I am waiting
for a religious revival
to sweep thru the state of Arizona
and I am waiting
for the Grapes of Wrath to be stored
and I am waiting
for them to prove
that God is really American

and I am waiting
to see God on television
piped onto church altars
if only they can find
the right channel
to tune in on
and I am waiting
for the Last Supper to be served again
with a strange new appetizer
and I am perpetually awaiting
a rebirth of wonder

I am waiting for my number to be called
and I am waiting
for the Salvation Army to take over
and I am waiting
for the meek to be blessed
and inherit the earth
without taxes
and I am waiting
for forests and animals
to reclaim the earth as theirs
and I am waiting
for a way to be devised
to destroy all nationalisms
without killing anybody
and I am waiting
for linnets and planets to fall like rain
and I am waiting for lovers and weepers
to lie down together again
in a new rebirth of wonder

I am waiting for the Great Divide to be crossed
and I am anxiously waiting
for the secret of eternal life to be discovered
by an obscure general practitioner
and I am waiting
for the storms of life

to be over
and I am waiting
to set sail for happiness
and I am waiting
for a reconstructed Mayflower
to reach America
with its picture story and tv rights
sold in advance to the natives
and I am waiting
for the lost music to sound again
in the Lost Continent
in a new rebirth of wonder

I am waiting for the day
that maketh all things clear
and I am awaiting retribution
for what America did
to Tom Sawyer
and I am waiting
for Alice in Wonderland
to retransmit to me
her total dream of innocence
and I am waiting
for Childe Roland to come
to the final darkest tower
and I am waiting
for Aphrodite
to grow live arms
at a final disarmament conference
in a new rebirth of wonder

I am waiting
to get some intimations
of immortality
by recollecting my early childhood
and I am waiting
for the green mornings to come again
youth's dumb green fields come back again

and I am waiting
for some strains of unpremeditated art
to shake my typewriter
and I am waiting to write
the great indelible poem
and I am waiting
for the last long careless rapture
and I am perpetually waiting
for the fleeing lovers on the Grecian Urn
to catch each other up at last
and embrace
and I am awaiting
perpetually and forever
a renaissance of wonder

AUTOBIOGRAPHY

I am leading a quiet life
in Mike's Place every day
watching the champs
of the Dante Billiard Parlor
and the French pinball addicts.
I am leading a quiet life
on lower East Broadway.
I am an American.
I was an American boy.
I read the American Boy Magazine
and became a boy scout
in the suburbs.
I thought I was Tom Sawyer
catching crayfish in the Bronx River
and imagining the Mississippi.
I had a baseball mit
and an American Flyer bike.
I delivered the Woman's Home Companion
at five in the afternoon
or the Herald Trib
at five in the morning.
I still can hear the paper thump
on lost porches.
I had an unhappy childhood.
I saw Lindbergh land.
I looked homeward
and saw no angel.
I got caught stealing pencils
from the Five and Ten Cent Store
the same month I made Eagle Scout.
I chopped trees for the CCC
and sat on them.
I landed in Normandy
in a rowboat that turned over.
I have seen the educated armies

on the beach at Dover.
I have seen Egyptian pilots in purple clouds
shopkeepers rolling up their blinds
at midday
potato salad and dandelions
at anarchist picnics.
I am reading 'Lorna Doone'
and a life of John Most
terror of the industrialist
a bomb on his desk at all times.
I have seen the garbagemen parade
in the Columbus Day Parade
behind the glib
farting trumpeters.
I have not been out to the Cloisters
in a long time
nor to the Tuileries
but I still keep thinking
of going.
I have seen the garbagemen parade
when it was snowing.
I have eaten hotdogs in ballparks.
I have heard the Gettysburg Address
and the Ginsberg Address.
I like it here
and I won't go back
where I came from.
I too have ridden boxcars boxcars boxcars.
I have travelled among unknown men.
I have been in Asia
with Noah in the Ark.
I was in India
when Rome was built.
I have been in the Manger
with an Ass.
I have seen the Eternal Distributor
from a White Hill
in South San Francisco

and the Laughing Woman at Loona Park
outside the Fun House
in a great rainstorm
still laughing.
I have heard the sound of revelry
by night.
I have wandered lonely
as a crowd.
I am leading a quiet life
outside of Mike's Place every day
watching the world walk by
in its curious shoes.
I once started out
to walk around the world
but ended up in Brooklyn.
That Bridge was too much for me.
I have engaged in silence
exile and cunning.
I flew too near the sun
and my wax wings fell off.
I am looking for my Old Man
whom I never knew.
I am looking for the Lost Leader
with whom I flew.
Young men should be explorers.
Home is where one starts from.
But Mother never told me
there'd be scenes like this.
Womb-weary
I rest
I have travelled.
I have seen goof city.
I have seen the mass mess.
I have heard Kid Ory cry.
I have heard a trombone preach.
I have heard Debussy
strained thru a sheet.
I have slept in a hundred islands

where books were trees.
I have heard the birds
that sound like bells.
I have worn grey flannel trousers
and walked upon the beach of hell.
I have dwelt in a hundred cities
where trees were books.
What subways what taxis what cafes!
What women with blind breasts
limbs lost among skyscrapers!
I have seen the statues of heroes
at carrefours.
Danton weeping at a metro entrance
Columbus in Barcelona
pointing Westward up the Ramblas
toward the American Express
Lincoln in his stony chair
And a great Stone Face
in North Dakota.
I know that Columbus
did not invent America.
I have heard a hundred housebroken Ezra Pounds.
They should all be freed.
It is long since I was a herdsman.
I am leading a quiet life
in Mike's Place every day
reading the Classified columns.
I have read the Reader's Digest
from cover to cover
and noted the close identification
of the United States and the Promised Land
where every coin is marked
In God We Trust
but the dollar bills do not have it
being gods unto themselves.
I read the Want Ads daily
looking for a stone a leaf
an unfound door.

I hear America singing
in the Yellow Pages.
One could never tell
the soul has its rages.
I read the papers every day
and hear humanity amiss
in the sad plethora of print.
I see where Walden Pond has been drained
to make an amusement park.
I see they're making Melville
eat his whale.
I see another war is coming
but I won't be there to fight it.
I have read the writing
on the outhouse wall.
I helped Kilroy write it.
I marched up Fifth Avenue
blowing on a bugle in a tight platoon
but hurried back to the Casbah
looking for my dog.
I see a similarity
between dogs and me.
Dogs are the true observers
walking up and down the world
thru the Molloy country.
I have walked down alleys
too narrow for Chryslers.
I have seen a hundred horseless milkwagons
in a vacant lot in Astoria.
Ben Shahn never painted them
but they're there
askew in Astoria.
I have heard the junkman's obbligato.
I have ridden superhighways
and believed the billboard's promises
Crossed the Jersey Flats
and seen the Cities of the Plain
And wallowed in the wilds of Westchester

with its roving bands of natives
in stationwagons.
I have seen them.
I am the man.
I was there.
I suffered
somewhat.
I am an American.
I have a passport.
I did not suffer in public.
And I'm too young to die.
I am a selfmade man.
And I have plans for the future.
I am in line
for a top job.
I may be moving on
to Detroit.
I am only temporarily
a tie salesman.
I am a good Joe.
I am an open book
to my boss.
I am a complete mystery
to my closest friends.
I am leading a quiet life
in Mike's Place every day
contemplating my navel.
I am a part
of the body's long madness.
I have wandered in various nightwoods.
I have leaned in drunken doorways.
I have written wild stories
without punctuation.
I am the man.
I was there.
I suffered
somewhat.
I have sat in an uneasy chair.

I am a tear of the sun.
I am a hill
where poets run.
I invented the alphabet
after watching the flight of cranes
who made letters with their legs.
I am a lake upon a plain.
I am a word
in a tree.
I am a hill of poetry.
I am a raid
on the inarticulate.
I have dreamt
that all my teeth fell out
but my tongue lived
to tell the tale.
For I am a still
of poetry.
I am a bank of song.
I am a playerpiano
in an abandoned casino
on a seaside esplanade
in a dense fog
still playing.
I see a similarity
between the Laughing Woman
and myself.
I have heard the sound of summer
in the rain.
I have seen girls on boardwalks
have complicated sensations.
I understand their hesitations.
I am a gatherer of fruit.
I have seen how kisses
cause euphoria.
I have risked enchantment.
I have seen the Virgin
in an appletree at Chartres

And Saint Joan burn
at the Bella Union.
I have seen giraffes in junglejims
their necks like love
wound around the iron circumstances
of the world.
I have seen the Venus Aphrodite
armless in her drafty corridor.
I have heard a siren sing
at One Fifth Avenue.
I have seen the White Goddess dancing
in the Rue des Beaux Arts
on the Fourteenth of July
and the Beautiful Dame Without Mercy
picking her nose in Chumley's.
She did not speak English.
She had yellow hair
and a hoarse voice
I am leading a quiet life
in Mike's Place every day
watching the pocket pool players
making the minestrone scene
wolfing the macaronis
and I have read somewhere
the Meaning of Existence
yet have forgotten
just exactly where.
But I am the man
And I'll be there.
And I may cause the lips
of those who are asleep
to speak.
And I may make my notebooks
into sheaves of grass.
And I may write my own
eponymous epitaph
instructing the horsemen
to pass.

DOG

The dog trots freely in the street
and sees reality
and the things he sees
are bigger than himself
and the things he sees
are his reality
Drunks in doorways
Moons on trees
The dog trots freely thru the street
and the things he sees
are smaller than himself
Fish on newsprint
Ants in holes
Chickens in Chinatown windows
their heads a block away
The dog trots freely in the street
and the things he smells
smell something like himself
The dog trots freely in the street
past puddles and babies
cats and cigars
poolrooms and policemen
He doesn't hate cops
He merely has no use for them
and he goes past them
and past the dead cows hung up whole
in front of the San Francisco Meat Market
He would rather eat a tender cow
than a tough policeman
though either might do
And he goes past the Romeo Ravioli Factory
and past Coit's Tower
and past Congressman Doyle of the Unamerican Committee
He's afraid of Coit's Tower
but he's not afraid of Congressman Doyle

although what he hears is very discouraging
very depressing
very absurd
to a sad young dog like himself
to a serious dog like himself
But he has his own free world to live in
His own fleas to eat
He will not be muzzled
Congressman Doyle is just another
fire hydrant
to him
The dog trots freely in the street
and has his own dog's life to live
and to think about
and to reflect upon
touching and tasting and testing everything
investigating everything
without benefit of perjury
a real realist
with a real tale to tell
and a real tail to tell it with
a real live
                barking
                        democratic dog
engaged in real
                free enterprise
with something to say
                        about ontology
something to say
                about reality
                        and how to see it
                                and how to hear it
with his head cocked sideways
                        at streetcorners
as if he is just about to have
                        his picture taken
                                for Victor Records
                listening for

                    His Master's Voice
        and looking
                like a living questionmark
                            into the
                                great gramophone
                            of puzzling existence
    with its wondrous hollow horn
            which always seems
        just about to spout forth
                            some Victorious answer
                                to everything

NEW YORK—ALBANY

God i had forgotten how
the Hudson burns
in indian autumn
Saugerties
Coxsackie
fall away through
all those trees
The leaves die turning
falling fallen
falling into loam of dark
yellow into death
Disappearing
falling fallen falling
those 'pestilence-stricken multitudes'
blown all blasted
They are hurting them
with wood rakes
They are raking them
in great hills
They are burning them
the leaves curl burning
the curled smoke gives up
to eternity
Never
never the same leaf turn again
the same leaves burn
In a red field
a white stallion stands
and pees his oblivion
upon those leaves

washing my bus window
only now blacked out
by a covered bridge
we flash through
only once
No roundtrip ticket
never returning
the youth years fallen
away back then
Under the Linden trees in Boston Common
Trees think
through these woods of years
They flame forever
with those thoughts
I did not see eternity
the other night
but now in burning
turning day
Every bush burns
Love licks
all down
All gone
in the red end
Small nuts fall
Mine too

EUPHORIA

As I approach the state of pure euphoria
  I find I need a largersize typewriter case
  to carry my underwear in
  and scars on my conscience
  are wounds imbedded in
  the gum eraser of my skin
  which still erases itself
As I approach the state of pure euphoria
  moon hides hot face in cool rice rain
  of Chinese painting
  and I cannot sleep because of the thunder
  under the summer afternoon
  in which a girl puts on a record of
  crazy attempts to play a saxophone
  punctuated by terrible forced laughter
  in another room
As I approach the state of pure euphoria
  they are building all the cities now
  on only one side of the street
  and my shoes walk up sides of buildings
  leaving tracks on windows
  with their soles of panes about to crack
  and shoe-tongues of roll-up shades alack
  I see my roll-up tongue upon a string
  and see my face upon the stick of it
  as on a pendulum about to swing
  a playing-card image with bound feet
  an upside-down hanged Villon
  And Mama recedes in a hand-held photo
  in a lost real-estate project ended in water
  Saratoga Avenue Yonkers
  where I now hang and swing
  on a last tree that stands drinking
  and where I'd still sing partsongs
  in a field of rapture

but an angel has me by the balls
and my castrato voice comes out too small
with a girl that puts a laughing record on
in another room
As I approach the state of pure euphoria
my eyes are gringo spies and I
may anytime be changed to birds
by a Tungus explosion that controls time
but I am no apocalyptic kid
and cannot sleep because of the thunder
under the summer afternoon
and my dumb bird's eye starts
out of my head
and flies around the world
in which a girl puts on
her record made of flesh
And I am animals without clothes
looking for a naked unity
but I'm divided up into countries
and I'm in Tibet on potato legs
and am a strange kind of clown
with befloured face and hair plastered down
and cannot sleep because of the thunder
under the needle my flesh turns under
She has turned it on
She has turned it over
She has turned me on
to play my other side
Her breasts bloom
figs burst
sun is white
I'll never come back
I wear Egyptian clothing

HIDDEN DOOR

(For Pablo Neruda, on the heights of Machu Picchu)

Hidden door dead secret
                which is Mother
Hidden door dead secret
                which is Father
Hidden door dead secret
                of our buried life
Hidden door behind which man carries
                his footprints along the streets
Hidden door of clay hands knocking
Hidden door without handles
                whose life is made of knocks
                by hand and foot
                Poor hand poor foot poor life!
Hidden door with hair for hinges
Hidden door with lips for latches
Hidden door with skeletons for keys
Hidden door autobiography of humanity
Hidden door dictionary of the universe
Hidden door palimpsest of myself
Hidden door I'm made of
                with my sticks of limbs
Hidden door pathetic fallacy
                of the evidence of the senses
                as to the nature of reality
Hidden door in blind eyes of termites
                that knock knock
Hidden door blind man with tin cup
                on a stone corner deaf and dumb
Hidden door train-whistle lost
                in book of night
Hidden door on night's wheels I blundering follow
                like a rhinoceros drinking through cities
Hidden door of carrier-pigeons' wings

121

                    which have half-forgotten
                    their destination
Hidden door plane's wing that skids in space
                    casting stone shadow
                    on sundial of earth
Hidden door flying boxcar of history
Hidden door of animal faces animal laughter animal dreams
                    and hidden door Cro-Magnon Man
                    among machines
                    and hidden door of his still uncollected
                    Collective Unconscious
Hidden door dark forest of America
                    knock knock in North Dakota
Hidden door that wings over America
                    and slants over San Francisco
                    and slams into the Pacific
                    drifting eternally southward
                    to Tierra del Fuego
                    with a knock knock undersea
                    at lost door of Lota coal mines
Hidden door surfboard to lost shore of light
                    and hidden door floated up on tides
                    like a shipwrecked coffinlid
                    bearing blind mouths blind breasts blind thought
                    through the centuries
Hidden door sea-angel cast-up Albatross
                    spouting seasperm of love in thirty languages
                    and the love-ship of life
                    sunk by the poison-squid of hate
Hidden door double-winged sticky-bird plumed serpent
                    stuck to moon afire forever drunk in time
                    flapping loose in eternity
Hidden door of the future mystic life
                    among Magellan's nebulae
                    and hidden door of my mislaid
                    visionary self

Hidden door San Luis rope-bridge which is man
           hung between nature and spirit
Hidden door of the spirit seen as a fleshy thing
           and hidden door of eyes and vulvas
           that still open only with a key
           of cartilage and flesh
           and hidden door frozen Inca mummy
           Prince of the Plomo
           fucked to death in sun-god sacrifice
Hidden door tin cup of blind brother mutes
           crouched on a Cuzco corner
           blowing bamboo flutes
           at coca midnight
Hidden door of the Andes at ten thousand feet
           in a ragged mist of ruins and red horizons
           with a seacoast hung below
           still lost among conquistadors
           horses dogs and incomprehensible laws
Hidden door wild river of the Urubamba
           upon which still floats somewhere
           the lost herb that separates soul from body
           and hidden door which is itself that herb
           and hidden door which is that separation
           and hidden door made of mirrors
           on the waters of this river
           in which I cannot see beyond myself
           because my body's in the way
Hidden door at last I see through
           beyond dear body bag of bones
           which I leave naked on a rock
Hidden door I wigless climb to
           beyond that river
Hidden door at last I fall through
           in the lost end of day
It is dusk
by the time we get to

Machu Picchu
Some Indians go by dancing
playing their flutes
and beating drums

(Peru-Chile, January–February, 1960)

OVERPOPULATION
¿No se puede vivir sin amor?

I must have misunderstood something
in this story
There must be a misprint
in this paper
Hats off! It says here
The final war is over
again
Here they come again
parading by
the café terrace
I stand on my chair to see
I still can't see
the brave burned hero's face
I stand on the table
waving my only hat
with the hole in it
I throw the hole away
into the street
after the black limousine
I don't throw my paper
I sit down with my paper
which has the explanation of everything
except there's a hole in it
Something missing in the story
where the hole is
Or I must have misunderstood something
The nations have decided
it says here
to abolish themselves at last
It's been decided at the highest level
and at the lowest level
to return to a primitive society
For science has conquered nature
but nature must not be conquered

So science must be abolished
and machines must go
after all their turning and turning
The automobile is a passing thing
after all
The horse is here to stay
Population has reached its limit
There's standingroom only
Nowhere
to lie down
anymore
Medicine must be abolished
so people can die
when they're supposed to
There's still room
under the surface
I keep hoping
I have misunderstood something
in this story
People still lose
and find themselves
in bed
and animals still
aren't as cruel as people
because they can't talk
but we weren't designed
to live forever and ever
and design is everything
The little enzyme they've extracted
that causes aging
must be lost in the body again
All must be begun over
in a new pastoral era
There've been too many advances
Life can't bear it
any longer
Life is not a drug
made from mushrooms

eaten by Samoyeds in Siberia
which fully retain
their intoxicating properties
when transmitted in urine
so that an endless line of men
may get drunk over and over
on the same mushroom
a chain reaction of avid statues
with mouths at penises
I must have misunderstood something
in this story
Life is intoxicating
but can't go on and on
putting on more and more
complicated clothes
hats girdles garterbelts
uplift bras lifting higher and higher
until they fly away
and breasts fall
after all
We've got to get naked again
it says here
though fornication's still illegal
in certain states
I must have misunderstood something
in this story
The world's no Klee mobile
and there must be an end
to all this rotation
around the goofball sun
The sun in its sic transit
barely clears the rooftops now
bumps over a Mobilgas Pegasus
and sinks behind my paper
with its hole
in which I keep hoping
I've misunderstood something
for Death is not the answer

to our problem
There must be some mistake—
There is—
The editorials say
we must do something
and we cannot do anything
For something's missing
where the hole is
sitting on the terrace
of this fancy coffeehouse
on the left side of the world
where I must
have misunderstood something
as a purple blond sweeps by
and one too-high tit pops out
and falls in my plate
I return it to her
without looking too embarrassed
This she takes as a good sign
She sits down
and gives me the other
wrapped in silk
I go on reading my paper
thinking I must
have misunderstood something
trying to look like
it's all happened before
It has
It's a clay mobile
with something missing
where the hole is
I look under the table and see
our legs are intertwined
Our two chairs fuse
Our arms are round each other
She's facing me
crouched in my lap
her legs around me

My white snake has entered her
speaks of love inside of her
She moans to hear it
But
something's missing
Sex without love
wears gay deceivers
I still have one of her breasts
in my hand
The waiter comes running
picks up my fallen paper
hoping he's misunderstood something
None of us will ever die
as long as this goes on
And the only way
to limit population
is to limit love?

UNDERWEAR

I didn't get much sleep last night
thinking about underwear
Have you ever stopped to consider
underwear in the abstract
When you really dig into it
some shocking problems are raised
Underwear is something
we all have to deal with
Everyone wears
some kind of underwear
The Pope wears underwear I hope
The Governor of Louisiana
wears underwear
I saw him on TV
He must have had tight underwear
He squirmed a lot
Underwear can really get you in a bind
You have seen the underwear ads
for men and women
so alike but so different
Women's underwear holds things up
Men's underwear holds things down
Underwear is one thing
men and women have in common
Underwear is all we have between us
You have seen the three-color pictures
with crotches encircled
to show the areas of extra strength
and three-way stretch
promising full freedom of action
Don't be deceived
It's all based on the two-party system
which doesn't allow much freedom of choice
the way things are set up
America in its Underwear

struggles thru the night
Underwear controls everything in the end
Take foundation garments for instance
They are really fascist forms
of underground government
making people believe
something but the truth
telling you what you can or can't do
Did you ever try to get around a girdle
Perhaps Non-Violent Action
is the only answer
Did Gandhi wear a girdle?
Did Lady Macbeth wear a girdle?
Was that why Macbeth murdered sleep?
And that spot she was always rubbing—
Was it really in her underwear?
Modern anglosaxon ladies
must have huge guilt complexes
always washing and washing and washing
Out damned spot
Underwear with spots very suspicious
Underwear with bulges very shocking
Underwear on clothesline a great flag of freedom
Someone has escaped his Underwear
May be naked somewhere
Help!
But don't worry
Everybody's still hung up in it
There won't be no real revolution
And poetry still the underwear of the soul
And underwear still covering
a multitude of faults
in the geological sense—
strange sedimentary stones, inscrutable cracks!
If I were you I'd keep aside
an oversize pair of winter underwear
Do not go naked into that good night
And in the meantime

keep calm and warm and dry
No use stirring ourselves up prematurely
'over Nothing'
Move forward with dignity
hand in vest
Don't get emotional
And death shall have no dominion
There's plenty of time my darling
Are we not still young and easy
Don't shout

COME LIE WITH ME AND
BE MY LOVE

Come lie with me and be my love

Love lie with me

Lie down with me

Under the cypress tree

In the sweet grasses

Where the wind lieth

Where the wind dieth

As night passes

Come lie with me

All night with me

And have enough of kissing me

And have enough of making love

And let our two selves speak

All night under the cypress tree

Without making love

ASSASSINATION RAGA

Tune in to a raga

on the stereo

and turn on Death TV

without its sound

Outside the plums are growing in a tree

'The force that through the green fuse

drives the flower'

drives Death TV

'A grief ago'

They lower the body soundlessly

into a huge plane in Dallas

into a huge plane in Los Angeles

marked 'United States of America'

and soundlessly

the 'United States of America'

takes off

& wings away with that Body

Tune out the TV sound

& listen soundlessly

to the blind mouths of its motors

& a sitar speaking on the stereo

a raga in a rage

at all that black death

and all that bad karma

La illaha el lill Allah

There is no god but God

The force that through the red fuze

drives the bullet

drives the needle in its dharma groove

and man the needle

drives that plane

of the 'United States of America'

through its sky full of shit & death

and the sky never ends

as it wings soundlessly

from those fucked-up cities

whose names we'd rather not remember

Inside the plane

inside the plane a wife

lies soundlessly

against the coffin

Engine whines as sitar sings outrageously

La illaha el lill Allah

There is no god but God?

There is no god but Death

The plums are falling through the tree

The force that drives the bullet

through the gun

drives everyone

as the 'United States of America'

flies on sightlessly

through the swift fierce years

with the dead weight of its Body

which they keep flying from Dallas

which they keep flying from Los Angeles

And the plane lands

without folding its wings

its shadow in mourning for itself

withdraws into itself

in death's draggy dominion

La illaha el lill Allah

There is no god but Death

The force that through the green fuze

drove his life

drives everyone

And they are driving the Body

they are driving the Body

up Fifth Avenue

past a million people in line

'We are going to be here a long time'

says Death TV's spielman

The cortège passes soundlessly

'Goodbye! Goodbye!' some people cry

The traffic flows around & on

The force that drives the cars

combusts our karma

La illaha el lill Allah

There is no god but Death

The force that drives our life to death

drives sitar too

so soundlessly

And they lift the Body

They lift the Body

of the United States of America

and carry it into a cathedral

singing Hallelujah He Shall Live

For ever & ever

And then the Body moves again

down Fifth Avenue

Fifty-seven black sedans after it

There are people with roses

behind the barricades

in bargain-basement dresses

And sitar sings & sings nonviolence

sitar sounds in us its images of ecstasy

its depth of ecstasy

against old dung & death

The force that strikes its strings

strikes us

And the funeral train

the silver train

starts up soundlessly

at a dead speed

over the hot land

an armed helicopter over it

They are clearing the tracks ahead of assassins

The tracks are lined with bare faces

A highschool band in New Brunswick plays

The Battle Hymn of the Republic

They have shot it down again

They have shot him down again

& will shoot him down again

& take him on a train

& lower him again

into a grave in Washington

Day & night journeys the coffin

through the dark land

too dark now to see the dark faces

Plums & planes are falling through the air

as sitar sings the only answer

sitar sings its only answer

sitar sounds the only sound

that still can still all violence

There is no god but Life

Sitar says it Sitar sounds it

Sitar sounds on us to love love & hate hate

Sitar breathes its Atman breath in us

sounds & sounds in us it lovely *om om*

At every step the pure wind rises

People with roses

behind the barricades!

First read, to an evening raga, at "The Incredible Poetry Reading," Nourse Auditorium, San Francisco, June 8, 1968, the day Robert Kennedy was buried.

"The force that through the green fuse drives the flower" & "A grief ago": from Dylan Thomas. "La illaha el lill Allah": variation of a Sufi ecstatic chant.

MOSCOW IN THE WILDERNESS, SEGOVIA IN THE SNOW

Midnight Moscow Airport
     sucks me in from Siberia
And blows me out alone
         in a black bus
     down dark straight night roads
      stark snow plains
       eternal taiga
         into monster Moscow
    stands of white birches
      ghosted in the gloaming
Where of a sudden
     Segovia bursts thru
        over the airwaves
They've let him in
       to drive the dark bus
Segovia's hands
        grasp the steering wheel
Yokels in housing projects
   drop their balalaikas & birch banjos
Segovia comes on
     like the pulse of life itself
Segovia comes on thru the snowdrifts
         and plains of La Mancha
    fields & fields & fields
      of frozen music
    melted on bus radios
Segovia at the instrument
     driving thru the night land
  of Antiquera
      Granada
       Seville
     Tracery of the Alhambra
    in a billion white birches
     born in the snow

                    trills of blackbirds in them
Segovia warms his hands
                    and melts Moscow
          moves his hand
                    with a circular motion
                         over an ivory bridge
                         to gutted Stalingrads
Segovia knows no answer
He's no Goya & he's no Picasso
but also
          he's no Sleeping Gypsy With Guitar
                    Guarded by a Lion
and who knows if he slept
                              with Franco
He knows black condors fly
He knows a free world when he hears one
His strums are runs upon it
He does not fret
He plucks his guts
and listens to himself as he plays
and speaks to himself
and echoes himself
And he keeps driving & driving
                              his instrument
     down the wide dark ways
                         into great Moscow
     down the black boulevards
               past Kremlin lit & locked
                    in its hard dream
               in the great Russian night
               past Bolshoi Ballet & Gorky Institute
                    John Reed at the Drama Theatre
                    Stalyagi & heroin at Taganka
Stone Mayakovsky stares
               thru a blizzard of white notes
                    in Russian winter light
Segovia hears his stoned cry
     and he hears the pulse in the blood

as he listens to life as he plays
and he keeps coming & coming
            thru the Russian winter night
He's in Moscow but doesn't know it
He played somewhere else
                and it comes out here
    in a thaw on an airwave
                over Gogol's Dark People
        stark figures
                in the white night streets
        clotted in the snow
He listens to them as he goes along
He listens for a free song
                such as he hardly hears
                back home
                Is Lenin listening
                    after fifty Octobers
Segovia walks thru the snow
                listening as he goes
        down Vorovsky Street
                    to the Writers' Union
He meets the old hairs that run it
    They dig him
            & they know what it means to dig
                in mahogany cities
Segovia teaches them open-tuning
    with which they can play anything
            freely & simply
    This is not his Master Class
He leaves them humming & goes on
Segovia plays in the loose snow
    and digs a bit alone
            under the free surface
                with his free hand
He strikes softly as he listens
He hears a dull thud
        where something is buried
        a familiar thud

such as he sometimes hears
back home
He turns away & goes on
down Vorovsky Street
His music has a longing sound
He yearns & yet does not yearn
He exists & is tranquil
in spite of all
He has no message
He is his own message
his own ideal sound
And he sounds so lonely to himself
as he goes on playing
in the iron-white streets
And he is saying: I say all I know
& I know no meaning
He is saying
This is the song of evening
when the sphinx lies down
This is the song of the day
that begins & begins
The night lifts
its white night-stick
The ash of life
dries my song
If you only knew
He is saying
My love my love
where are you
Under the pomegranate tree
He is saying
Where is joy where is ecstasy
stretched out in the snow
where only the birds are at home
He is saying
There's a huge emptiness here
that stares from all the faces
All that is lost must be

              looked for once more
He is saying
       Far from me far from me
       you are the hour & the generation
       they marked for result
He is saying
       I am your ruin
          unique & immortal
      am your happiness unknown
      . am light
          where you are dark
          where you are heavy
He is saying
       I am an old man
       and life flowers
            in the windows of the sun
     But where is the sun the sun
              Soleares . . .
On the steps of a jail
       that looks like a church
          he finds a white bird
What is important in life? says the bird
Segovia says Nada but keeps on playing
       his Answer
And he cries out now
       when he sees a strange woman
          or sees a strange thing
       And he hears many strange women
          & many strange things
          after fifty Octobers
          & fifty strange springs
And Segovia follows them
       down their streets
       and into their houses
       and into their rooms
       and into the night of their beds
      And waits for them to make love
      And waits for them to speak

>   And waits & waits for them to speak
And he cries out now
>   when he hears them speak
>   at last in their last retreat
No he doesn't cry out
He never cries out
He is taciturn & never sings
Only his instrument speaks & sings
But when it does sing
when it does cry out
at what it hears
>   an ancient armadillo
>   asleep for centuries
>   in the cellar of the Kremlin
>   raises its horny head
>   opens its square third eye
> and looks around blinking
>   and then at last
>   unglues its great gut mouth
>   and utters
>   ecstatic static

Moscow-San Francisco, March, 1967

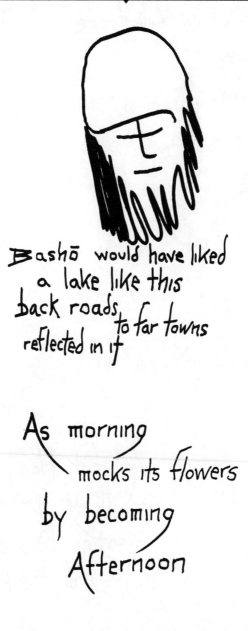

Bashō would have liked
a lake like this
back roads
to far towns
reflected in it

As morning
mocks its flowers
by becoming
Afternoon

And when the white furze
     stands up
   on the dandelion stem
      it is time
                to blow

Ah day is done
              Day
        is done
   And fish float
       through the trees
     eating the seeds
              of the sun

Papyrus and bamboo
in the window's weather—
East + West's leaves
tangled together

Sunlight casts its leaves
upon the wall
Wind stirs them
even
in the closed room

Last night a longing
a roaring in a sea shell
a confused murmur
of birds + men

And bodies
were boats

A flutter of wings
Sound and weeping
fill the air
And the quivering
meat wheel
turns

TRUE CONFESSIONAL

I was conceived in the summer of Nineteen Eighteen
(or was it Thirty Eight)
when some kind of war was going on
but it didn't stop two people
from making love in Ossining that year
I like to think on a riverbank in sun
on a picnic by the Hudson
as in a painting of the Hudson River School
or up at Bear Mountain maybe
after taking the old Hudson River Line
paddlewheel excursion steamer
(I may have added the paddlewheel—
the Hudson my Mississippi)
And on the way back she
already carried me
inside of her
I lawrence ferlinghetti
wrought from the dark in my mother long ago
born in a small back bedroom—
In the next room my brother heard
the first cry,
many years later wrote me—
"Poor Mom—No husband—No money—Pop dead—
How she went through it all—"
Someone squeezed my heart
to make it go
I cried and sprang up
Open eye open heart where
do I wander
into the heart of the world

151

Carried away
by another I knew not
And which of me shall know my brother?
'I am my son, my mother, my father,
I am born of myself
my own flesh sucked'
And someone squeezed my heart
to make me go
And I began to go
through my number
I was a wind-up toy
someone had dropped wound-up
into a world already
running down
The world had been going on
a long time already
but it made no difference
It was new it was like new
i made it new
i saw it shining
and it shone in the sun
and it spun in the sun
and the skein it spun
was pure light
My life was made of it
made of the skeins of light
The cobwebs of Night
were not on it
were not of it
It was too bright
to see
too luminous too numinous
to cast a shadow
and there was another world
behind the bright screens
I had only to close my eyes
for another world to appear
too near and too dear

to be anything but myself
my inside self
where everything real
was to happen
in this place which still exists
inside myself
and hasn't changed that much
certainly not as much
as the outside
with its bag of skin
and its 'aluminum beard'
and its blue blue eyes
which see as one eye
in the middle of the head
where everything happens
except what happens
in the heart
vajra lotus diamond heart
wherein I read
the poem that never ends

MOCK CONFESSIONAL

Fish-sky at morning
and why should I
tell the world about it
It's not the kind of news
makes headlines down here
Anyway I hear people are wondering about me
and I've written this to clear the air
especially since
people who read my books
don't read other books
I'm sometimes known as the creator
of the immortal line
'When I was a boy I was my father'
I generally feel like kissing someone
when I'm asleep
I don't like sweet wine and cigarettes
police and bitchy women
Otherwise I'm amenable
to what goes down out here
I know I'll never amount to anything
I don't want to amount to
which is not to say I'm without ambition
Sometimes I feel a fluttering in me
and I may sometime fly into the sun
wearing wax wings
I have a feeling I'm falling
on rare occasions
but most of the time I have my feet on the ground
I can't help it if the ground itself is falling
I sometimes wonder what my totem animal is
In any case I'm not a crow or a grey fox
I may be somewhere between a centaur
and Sancho Panza's ass
I know a good thing when I see it

and intend to survive
even if it means being a survivor
I have strange dreams sometimes
but they're not half as weird as
what I see walking down the street
I never did like people who walk like
they're on their way to a party
When I'm at cocktail parties
I usually don't say what I'm thinking
which results in the usual drunkenness
I can't help it if Catholic priests
won't accept my confession
that I consider the Immaculate Conception
a cock-and-bull story
and always viewed the world as a *mons veneris*
After all Father
there must have been plans
for more than two Comings
If this sounds like bright cocktail chatter
remember I'm drinking out of desperation
I believe in the Revolution
in its double-edged image
but baby yours is not mine
I refuse to confess to the boys
or the ladies in the bathroom
What could they be up to
which I am not up to
Why don't we all just dance and sing
and let the appendages hang out where they will
Let's forge on to simpler things
The last time I saw Paris
was in the winter of 1967
when I had to sleep in a windowless room
in a street whose name I'd rather not remember
since I insisted in staying in the same hotel
I'd stayed in as a student a century ago
which now was made over into a mattress factory

Some days I just don't know what to make of things
Other days I'm sure I have the solution to everything
the little key that will fit everything
and turn everything to my own alchemy
if not the wooden key that mayors give you
Well I'll have to begin again
It seems my personal life is a complete
mystery even to myself
though I'm a raving success in the field
While I'm catching the high fly
a worm has succeeded in eating
a hole in my soul
When I reach down to mend it
I find a cocoon in my crotch
which becomes a butterfly as I watch
While I'm zipping up
it flits to my heart
And the world begins again
With a lurch it starts whirling once more
with its little supercargo of flesh
The race horses in their slots
take off again
but the big board registers Tilt
when someone like the government
jiggles the machine
and my key won't fit my own door anymore
but that's still no sign I'm not an artistic triumph
I've proved that already with my fearless pen
though now it may run dry
and I have to dip it in some body fluid to continue
of which there are only two symbolic choices:
blood or water
The moving finger writes in both
and fumbles on
but leaves its indelible traces
only in one
which makes me wonder

if I really choose to be immortal
Excuse me for a moment
There's another butterfly
lighted on my fly
and my metamorphosis
may not be done
though now I am 'old'
and am my son

THE ASTONISHED HEART

She of the shining eyes
in the next booth
Ramada Inn Lawrence Kansas
Beautiful teeth and long hair
talking to a smiler in sharkskin
She is twenty and aglow
saying something important
about their life together
It must be serious
the way she looks at him
with her far-eyed look
half-smiling
or maybe it is just about the tragedy
of some movie she's just been to
I can't hear the words
Just the voice lisping a little
flat almost
except for the eyes
He smiles into them
They are both smiling
into each other
Maybe it is just a little joke
between them
not a tragedy at all
There is nothing to do about it
in either case
Just watch it happen
amazed and aghast
at the fantastic craziness of it
and of existence
which just goes on
bowling us over
Set 'em up in the other alley
Wow watch this one
I got my crystal spectacles on

Soon soon their supper will come
Soon soon they will eat it
or each other
not necessarily a tragedy
She is giving him her
long look again
Soon the curious plastic-antique restaurant
will curl up around them
and blow away with them
over the plains of Kansas
not necessarily
an ecological tragedy
Maybe it is all just a goofy movie
about eating
He may be about to eat a fish
whose baked eye glares up at him
Soon soon they will devour each other
Eyes feasting on each other
each prepares the other's surrender
Soon she will look away
with her long look
out a window
through the Standard Station's neons
toward the plains
where somewhere soon
they will lie together hot
under the sun at noon
Soon soon she will finish eating
her appetizer
Soon soon she will look at him again
You can tell she's still hungry
Woman is a wonderful invention
of man
And man a wonderful invention
of woman
Soon soon they will be born again in the sun
Soon too soon they will be wonderfully done
with each other

She looks away from him now
into the great American night
and seems to see very far
unless it's just contact lenses
making her eyes
so shiny
There is a great crowded bluff
in Lawrence Kansas
that looks a long way
into the astonished heart
of America

SUEÑO REAL

1.

In the eternal dream-time
                a fish dreamt ocean
                a bird sky
And I stand on the beach in the land
        where all is still frontier
And hold an aluminum bird in my hand
And don't dream sand
                running through my head
                        as through an hourglass

2.

In the eternal dream-time
   a sigh
            falls from the sky
   from some other history than our own
                as if the world were almost
                brand new

3.

Ah, como la tierra es buena
   y la vida—
            la vida es sueño real . . .
Sun on fire
            sucked into ocean
        And the only shadow
                    the shadow of desire afire

4.

                    In the eternal dream-time
a whale of a man

                    in a great round
                                        Mexican sombrero
              with a wide-open
                                        painted eye on it
suddenly appears
                    on the beach by the woods
        The sun
                    casts his shadow
                                        on the ground

                                5.

Back at the cabin in the woods by the stream
        the white copy of Venus Aphrodite
            stands silent on the porch
        Silk cobwebs on her
                    glisten and quiver in wind
                    lyre-strands strung
                                from head to shoulder
The stream below
                        sheds its multi-murmuring
            A million
                    spirit-voices
                undertone to birds
                            in lush trees above
        A bee browses
                        on the alabaster breasts
                and moves
                            to the very mouth of Venus
                    who is no longer a copy
Ah, aaah
                the universe breathes
A bat
            scrunches up
                        under the eaves

162

6.

Loony surrealist dream
    of a lead soldier in a
            tin cowboy hat
     riding over
        the burnt horizon
       backwards on his horse
In his hand he holds
        a small white horse
      bearing a small white cowboy
           between its teeth
And this cowboy is singing
          'Life is a real dream'

7.

And I went out in the dark dawn
  in the morning of the world
    in the first morning
     and saw the Northern Cross
      with a slow thrust
        bury itself in the mountain
         and burn there in white fire
   huge Excalibur
        stuck in stone

8.

What is that bird
        trying to call my attention?
I've been fifty years
      waiting for this moment
       of light
And he took it

9.

I know that I don't dream
    'Life

        dreams me'
It is life
    that dreams around me
The leaves breathe
        the hills
            breathe
There is a willow aflame
          with sun
There are a series
    of waterproof mouths
And my words are
      myself. . . .

10.

Transliteration of inanimate objects
    into real beings . . .
        a palimpsest
          an illegible
            manuscreed
        Braille
          night-thought spoke
by a stream impossible
      to decipher. . . .

AN ELEGY ON THE DEATH
OF KENNETH PATCHEN

A poet is born
A poet dies
And all that lies between
is us
and the world

And the world lies about it
making as if it had got his message
even though it is poetry
but most of the world wishing
it could just forget about him
and his awful strange prophecies

Along with all the other strange things
he said about the world
which were all too true
and which made them fear him
more than they loved him
though he spoke much of love
Along with all the alarms he sounded
which turned out to be false
if only for the moment
all of which made them fear his tongue
more than they loved him
Though he spoke much of love
and never lived by 'silence exile & cunning'
and was a loud conscientious objector to
the deaths we daily give each other
though we speak much of love
And when such a one dies
even the agents of Death should take note
and shake the shit from their wings
in Air Force One

But they do not
And the shit still flies

And the poet now is disconnected
                    and won't call back
    though he spoke much of love

And still we hear him say
              'Do I not deal with angels
                  when her lips I touch'
And still we hear him say
                  'O my darling troubles heaven
                    with her loveliness'
And still we love to hear him say
    'As we are so wonderfully done with each other
    We can walk into our separate sleep
    On floors of music where the milkwhite cloak
                    of childhood lies'
And still we hear him saying
        'Therefore the constant powers do not lessen.
        Nor is the property of the spirit scattered
        on the cold hills of these events'
And still we hear him asking
        'Do the dead know what time it is?'

He is gone under
                    He is scattered
                                    undersea
        and knows what time
                    but won't be back to tell it
He would be too proud to call back anyway
    And too full of strange laughter
                    to speak to us anymore anyway
And the weight of human experience
            lies upon the world
    like the chains of the sea
                            in which he sings
And he swings in the tides of the sea
    And his ashes are washed
            in the ides of the sea

And 'an astonished eye looks out of the air'
              to see the poet singing there

And dusk falls down a coast somewhere

   where a white horse without a rider
         turns its head
                  to the sea

*First read at the City Lights Poets Theatre Kenneth Patchen Memorial
Reading, February 3, 1972, San Francisco*

THE MAN WHO RODE AWAY

(*To D. H. Lawrence*)

Above Taos now
                        I peer through the crack
        of your locked door
                        Dead Lawrence
and there indeed I see
                        they've got you now at last
        safely stashed away
                        locked away from the light
        of your dear sun
                        in the weird great dark
        of your little
                        shuttered shrine
with the dark brown cover
                        of your old portable
clenched like a jaw upon
                        dumb keys
                                teeth sans tongue
        as in a mute mask
                        of a Greek megaphone

        Ah here's real proof
                        the soul has its rages—
                dampered!
                        in darkness!
        shrine locked—
                        booby-trapped for burglars—
plumed serpent stoned
                        into a gargoyle!

Lawrence Lawrence bearded David
                        Phoenix flamed
        out of a mine-head
                        ash to ash
        Sown in Vence
                        and resown in America

(del Norte)
                        Where now
            here now
                        your portable seed
        has blown away
                        Other seeds
        are growing
                        Not yours
            Lawrence
                        in the white sands
                                proving grounds!

Lawrence now I see you come alone
from your cribbed cabin
all fenced in the backyard compound
of that big caretaker's house

You stand still a moment in the still air.

Your eyes have a Mexican look
turned South
over the arroyos
ahora y siempre

Winter is coming

You have your ticket

You have your blue denim jacket

You have your crazy Stetson

Your tin phoenix tacked to a tree
drops in a giftshop window

A mistral wind
rattles the pine needles
of your bones

POEM FOR OLD WALT

SPRING DUSK DARK SHORE
LONG ISLAND NEW YORK APRIL
SKY OVER PATCHOGUE DENSE & GREY
AS WHITMAN'S BEARD
FLIGHTS OF GREY GEESE
NESTED IN IT
OVER HULK OF HIS FAIR BODY—
'FISH-SHAPE PAUMANOK'—
HULK OF HIM HOVE-TO
OFF OLD MANNAHATTA—
POETS STILL
SWIM OFF OF IT
THEIR FAR CRIES FAILING
LIKE LOST SAILORS IN A BURNING
TURNER SHIPWRECK
RED SUN FLAMES THROUGH
ON THE VERY SHORES OF LIGHT

AN IMAGINARY HAPPENING, LONDON

In the lower left-hand corner
of an album landscape
I am walking thru a dark park
with a noted nymphomaniac
trying to discover
for what she is noted

We are talking as we walk
of various villainies
of church & state
and of the tyrannies
of love & hate

The moon makes hairless nudes

An alabaster girl upon her back
becomes a body made of soap
beneath a wet gypsy

Suddenly we rush
thru a bent gate
into the hot grass

One more tree
falls in the forest

THOUGHTS TO A CONCERTO
OF TELEMANN

'The curious upward stumbling motion
of the oboe d'amore'
must be love itself among the strands
of emotion. It is as if its motion
were not its own at all,
as if these hands
had never struck those strings
we sing to,
swing to
(as puppets do, unbroken)
as if we never really meant to
be so strung to
those sweet pitches
love so frets us to
so tautly
so mutely
(love's bodies laid like harps!)
and then as if
there never were still more
unspoken,
as if dumb mind did never grieve
among the woodwinds,
as if its chords
did never quiver anymore
as in a buried mandolin,
as if that love
were hardly in it
anymore,
nor sounded in it
anymore,
nor heart hear it
nor life bear it
anymore.
Yet it does, it does!

CRO-MAGNONS

Cro-Magnons carried stones for books
And a flat dark stone I came upon
was one in which I read
the carbon copy histories
of creepy man
in the fine print of fossils pressed
between the stone's aged pages
the first syllables of recorded time
made into burning messages
about the first decline and fall
and the dissent of species

so that
when I cracked it open I surprised
the shadow of a lizard on the steps
of an Alexandrian branch library
burning on the broken stone
in a bright daze of sunlight
And in a flicker of that lizard's loose tongue
in one cooled instant of carbonized time
deciphered eternity

POUND AT SPOLETO

I walked into a loge in the Teatro Melisso, the lovely Renaissance salle where the poetry readings and the chamber concerts were held every day of the Spoleto Festival, and suddenly saw Ezra Pound for the first time, still as a mandarin statue in a box in a balcony at the back of the theatre, one tier up from the stalls. It was a shock, seeing only a striking old man in a curious pose, thin and long haired, aquiline at 80, head tilted strangely to one side, lost in permanent abstraction. . . . After three younger poets on stage, he was scheduled to read from his box, and there he sat with an old friend (who held his papers) waiting. He regarded the knuckles of his hands, moving them a very little, expressionless. Only once, when everyone else in the full theatre applauded someone on stage, did he rouse himself to clap, without looking up, as if stimulated by sound in a void. . . . After almost an hour, his turn came. Or after a life. . . . Everyone in the hall rose, turned and looked back and up at Pound in his booth, applauding. The applause was prolonged and Pound tried to rise from his armchair. A microphone was partly in the way. He grasped the arms of the chair with his boney hands and tried to rise. He could not and he tried again and could not. His old friend did not try to help him. Finally she put a poem in his hand, and after at least a minute his voice came out. First the jaw moved and then the voice came out, inaudible. A young Italian pulled the mike up very close to his face and held it there and the voice came over, frail but stubborn, higher than I had expected, a thin, soft monotone. The hall had gone silent at a stroke. The voice knocked me down, so soft, so thin, so frail, so stubborn still. I put my head on my arms on the velvet sill of the box. I was surprised to see a single tear drop on my knee. The thin, indomitable voice went on. I went blind from the box, through the back door of it, into the empty corridor of the theatre where they still sat turned to him, went down and out, into the sunlight, weeping. . . .

    Up above the town
                by the ancient aqueduct
       the chestnut trees
               were still in bloom

Mute birds
        flew in the valley
                far below
   The sun shone
            on the chestnut trees
and the leaves
        turned in the sun
     and turned and turned and turned
     And would continue turning
His voice
     went on
        and on
             through the leaves. . . .

THIRD WORLD CALLING

This loud morning
sensed a small cry in
the news
paper
caught somewhere on
an inner page
I
decide to travel for lunch &
end up in an automat
White House Cafeteria
looking thru a little window
put a nickle in the slot
and out comes
fried rice
Taking a tour
of the rest of that building
I hear a small cry
beyond the rice paddies
between floors where
the escalator sticks
and remember last night's dream of
attending my own funeral
at a drive-in mortuary
not really believing
I was that dead
Someone throwing rice
All the windows dry
Tipped the coffin open & laughed
into it
and out falls
old funnyface
myself
the bargain tragedian
with a small cry

followed by sound of Che Guevara singing
    in the voice of Fidel

Far over the Perfume River
                    the clouds pass
        carrying small cries
The monsoon has set in
            the windows weep

      I
        back up to
                the Pentagon
     on a flatbed truck
and unload the small brown bodies
            fresh from the blasted fields!

BASEBALL CANTO

Watching baseball
sitting in the sun
eating popcorn
reading Ezra Pound
and wishing Juan Marichal
would hit a hole right through
the Anglo-Saxon tradition
in the First Canto
and demolish the barbarian invaders
When the San Francisco Giants take the field
and everybody stands up to the National Anthem
with some Irish tenor's voice
piped over the loudspeakers
with all the players struck dead in their places
and the white umpires like Irish cops
in their black suits and little black caps
pressed over their hearts
standing straight and still
like at some funeral of a blarney bartender
and all facing East
as if expecting some Great White Hope
or the Founding Fathers
to appear on the horizon
like 1066 or 1776 or all that
But Willie Mays appears instead
in the bottom of the first
and a roar goes up
    as he clouts the first one into the sun
      and takes off
        like a footrunner from Thebes
    The ball is lost in the sun
      and maidens wail after him
      but he keeps running
        through the Anglo-Saxon epic
 And Tito Fuentes comes up

looking like a bullfighter
in his tight pants and small pointed shoes

And the rightfield bleachers go mad
with chicanos & blacks & Brooklyn beerdrinkers
"Sweet Tito! Sock it to heem, Sweet Tito!"
And Sweet Tito puts his foot in the bucket
and smacks one that don't come back at all
and flees around the bases
like he's escaping from the United Fruit Company
as the gringo dollar beats out the Pound
and Sweet Tito beats it out
like he's beating out usury
not to mention fascism and anti-semitism
And Juan Marichal comes up
and the chicano bleachers go loco again
as Juan belts the first fast ball
out of sight
and rounds first and keeps going
and rounds second and rounds third
and keeps going
and hits pay-dirt
to the roars of the grungy populace
As some nut presses the backstage panic button
for the tape-recorded National Anthem again
to save the situation
but it don't stop nobody this time
in their revolution round the loaded white bases
in this last of the great Anglo-Saxon epics
in the *Territorio Libre* of baseball

RECIPE FOR HAPPINESS IN
KHABAROVSK OR ANYPLACE

One grand boulevard with trees
with one grand café in sun
with strong black coffee in very small cups

One not necessarily very beautiful
man or woman who loves you

One fine day

THE JACK OF HEARTS
(*For Dylan*)

Who are we now, who are we ever,
Skin books parchment bodies libraries of the living
gilt almanachs of the very rich
encyclopedias of little people
packs of players face down
on faded maps of America
with no Jack of Hearts
in the time of the ostrich
Fields full of rooks
dumb pawns in black-and-white kingdoms
And revolutions the festivals of the oppressed
and festivals the little revolutions
of the bourgeoisie
where gypsy fortune tellers deal
without the Jack of Hearts
the black-eyed one who sees all ways
the one with the eye of a horse
the one with the light in his eye
the one with his eye on the star named Nova
the one for the ones with no one to lead them
the one whose day has just begun
the one with the star in his cap
the cat with future feet
looking like a Jack of Hearts
mystic Jack Zen Jack with crazy koans
Vegas Jack who rolls the bones
the high roller behind the dealer
the one who'll shake them
the one who'll shake the ones unshaken

the fearless one
the one without bullshit
the stud with the straightest answer
the one with blazing words for guns
the distance runner with the word to pass
the night rider with the urgent message
The man from La Mancha riding bareback
The one who bears the great tradition
and breaks it
The Mysterious Stranger who comes & goes
The Jack of Hearts who speaks out
in the time of the ostrich
the one who sees the ostrich
the one who sees what the ostrich sees in the sand
the one who digs the mystery
and stands in the corner smiling
like a Jack of Hearts
at the ones with no one to lead them
the ones with their eyes in the sands
the sand that runs through the glass
the ones who don't want to look
at what's going down around them
the shut-eye ones who wish
that someone else would seize the day
that someone else would tell them
which way up and which way out
and whom to hate and whom to love
like Big Jack groovy Jack the Jack of light
Sainted Jack who had the Revelations
and spoke the poem of apocalypse
Poet Jack with the light pack
who travels by himself
and leaves the ladies smiling
Dharma Jack with the beatitudes
drunk on a bus addressing everyone
the silent ones with the frozen faces
the ones with *The Wall Street Journal*
who never speak to strangers

the ones that got lost in the shuffle
and never drew the Jack of Hearts
the one who'd turn them on
who'd save them from themselves
the one who heals the Hamlet in them
the silent Ham who never acts
the dude on the corner in two-tone shoes
who knows the name of the game
and names his game
the kid who paints the fence
the boy who digs the treasure up
the boy with the beans on the beanstalk
the dandy man the candy man
the one with the lollipops
the harlequin man
who tells the tic-toc man to stuff it
in front of the house that Jack built
behind the house that Jack built
where sleeps the Cock that crowed in the morn
where sleeps the Cow with the crumpled horn
where sleeps the dude who kept the horse
with the beautiful form
and kissed the Maiden all forlorn
the Jack of the pack all tattered and torn
the one the queen keeps her eye on
Dark Rider on a white horse
after the Apocalypse
Prophet stoned on the wheel of fortune
Sweet singer with harp half-hid
who speaks with the cry of cicadas
who tells the tale too truly
for the ones with no one to tell them
the true tale of sound and fury
the Jack of Hearts who lays it out
who tells it as it is
the one who wears no watch
yet tells the time too truly
and reads the Knight of Cups

and knows himself
the Knave of Hearts the Jack of Hearts
who stole the tarts
of love & laughter
the Jack who tells his dream
to those with no one to dream it
the one who tells his dream
to the hard-eyed innocents
and lays it out for the blind hippie
the black dream the white dream
of the Jack of Hearts
whose skeleton is neither black nor white
the long dream the dream of heads & hearts
the trip of hearts the flip of hearts
that turns the Hanged Man right side up
and saves the Drowned Sailor
with the breath of love
the wet dream the hard dream the sweet dream
of the Deck Hand on the tall ship sailing softly
Blackjack yellowjack the steeplejack
who sets the clock in the tower
and sees the chimes of freedom flashing
his only watch within him
the high one the turned-on one the tuned-in one
the one who digs
in the time of the ostrich
and finds the sun-stone
of himself
the woman-man
the whole man
who holds all worlds together
when all is said and all is done
in the wild eye the wide eye
of the Jack of Hearts
who stands in a doorway
clothed in sun

DIRECTOR OF ALIENATION

Looking in the mirrors at Macy's
and thinking it's a subterranean plot
to make me feel like Chaplin
snuck in with his bent shoes & beat bowler
looking for a fair-haired angel
Who's this bum
crept in off the streets
blinking in the neon
an anarchist among the floorwalkers
a strike-breaker even
right past the pickets
and the picket line is the People yet?
I think I'll hook a new derby
with my cane
and put a sign on it reading
Director of Alienation
or The Real Revolution
So it's Mister Alienation is it
like he don't like nobody?
It's not me It's Them out of step
I came in looking for an angel
male or female dark or fair
but why does everyone look
so serious or unhappy
like as if everyone's alienated
from something or someone
from the whole earth even
and the green land
among the loud indignant birds
My land is your land
but 'all is changed, changed utterly'
Look at this alien face
in this elevator mirror
The Tele-tector scans me
He looks paranoid Better get him out

before he starts trying on the underwear
Keep your filthy mitts offa
I better stick to the escalators
Too many nylon ladies in the lifts
too many two-way mirrors
I came in looking for an angel
among the alien corn
I might get caught
fingering the lingerie
feeling up the manikins
House dicks after me
Where's your credit cards
They'll find the hole in my sock
in the Shoe Department
The full-length mirrors all designed
to make you look your worst
so you'll get real depressed
and throw off your old clothes
and buy new duds on the spot
Well I'll take them at their word
They asked for it
Off with these grungy threads
and slide down the escalators bare-ass
Slip between the on-sale sheets
into the on-sale bed
feeling for an angel in it
Try this new flush toilet
and the portable shower
emerging from the bath in something sexy
into a store window
among the Coquette Wigs by Eva Gabor
and freeze in one of the wigs
when the Keystone Cops come running
I came in looking for an angel
passion eyes and longing hair
in mirrors made of water
But what's this wrack of civilization
I've fallen into

This must be the end of something
the last days of somebody's empire
Seven floors of it
from Women's Wear to Men's Furnishings
Lost souls descending thru
Dante's seven circles
Ladies like bees avaricious
clustered at counters
I don't want to join them either
Always the Outsider
What a drag
Why don't you get with it
It's your country
What a cliché this Outsider
a real bore
But is there anyone left inside
in this year of the boring Bicentennial
Indians alienated Artists alienated
All these poets alienated
Parents husbands wives alienated
Kids alienated
Even billionaires alienated
hiding out in foreign countries
Don't let them tell you different
with their flags and their grants
So Buy Buy Buy
and get Inside
Get a loada this junk
You wanna belong
You gotta have it
Pull yourself together
and descend to Macy's basement
And eat your way up
thru the seven stages
of this classless society
with the Credit Department on the top floor
where surely some revelation is at hand
Consume your way up

until you're consumed by it
at the very top
where surely a terrible beauty is born
Then jump off the roof
o dark of hair
o Ruth among the alien porn
waving plastic jewels and genitals

WILD DREAMS OF A NEW BEGINNING

There's a breathless hush on the freeway tonight
Beyond the ledges of concrete
restaurants fall into dreams
with candlelight couples
Lost Alexandria still burns
in a billion lightbulbs
Lives cross lives
idling at stoplights
Beyond the cloverleaf turnoffs
'Souls eat souls in the general emptiness'
A piano concerto comes out a kitchen window
A yogi speaks at Ojai
'It's all taking place in one mind'
On the lawn among the trees
lovers are listening
for the master to tell them they are one
with the universe
Eyes smell flowers and become them
There's a deathless hush
on the freeway tonight
as a Pacific tidal wave a mile high
                              sweeps in
Los Angeles breathes its last gas
and sinks into the sea like the *Titanic* all lights lit
Nine minutes later Willa Cather's Nebraska
                              sinks with it
The seas come in over Utah
Mormon tabernacles washed away like salt
Coyotes are confounded & swim nowhere
An orchestra onstage in Omaha
keeps on playing Handel's *Water Music*
Horns fill with water
and bass players float away on their instruments
clutching them like lovers horizontal
Chicago's Loop becomes a rollercoaster

Skyscrapers filled like water glasses
Great Lakes mixed with Buddhist brine
Great Books watered down in Evanston
Milwaukee beer topped with sea foam
Beau Fleuve of Buffalo suddenly become salt
Manhattan Island swept clean in sixteen seconds
buried masts of New Amsterdam arise
as the great wave sweeps on Eastward
to wash away over-age Camembert Europe
Mannahatta steaming in sea-vines
the washed land awakes again to wilderness
the only sound a vast thrumming of crickets
a cry of seabirds high over
in empty eternity
as the Hudson retakes its thickets
and Indians reclaim their canoes

LOST PARENTS

It takes a fast car
                to lead a double life
in these days of short-distance love affairs
    when he has far-out lovers in
                        three different locations
    and a date with each one
                at least twice a week
    a little simple arithmetic shows
            what a workout he's engaged in
crossing & recrossing the city
        from bedroom to patio to swimming pool
the ignition key hot
        and the backseat a jumble of clothes
                            for different life-styles
a surfboard on the roof
        and a copy of Kahlil Gibran or Rod McKuen
                        under the dashboard
            next to the Indian music casettes
        packs of Tarot and the I-Ching
                    crammed into the glove compartment
        along with old traffic tickets
                    and hardpacks of Kents
            dents attesting to the passion
                        of his last lover
And his answering service
            catching him on the freeway
                    between two calls or two encounter groups
        and the urgent message left
        with an unlisted number to call Carol
        about the bottle of fine wine
            he forgot to pick up
                and deliver to the gallery
                    for the reception at nine
While she shuttles to her gynecologist
        and will meet him later

                    between two other numbers
                                    male or female
            including his wife
                who also called twice
        wanting to know where he's been
                and what he's done
                            with their throw-away children
            who
                left to their own devices
                    in a beach house at Malibu
            grew up and dropped out into Nothing
                    in a Jungian search
                                for lost parents
                                    their own age

PEOPLE GETTING DIVORCED

People getting divorced
    riding around with their clothes in the car
and wondering what happened
      to everyone and everything
      including their other
        pair of shoes
   And if you spy one
    then who knows what happened
      to the other
      with tongue alack
and years later not even knowing
     if the other ever
      found a mate
     without splitting the seams
     or remained intact
       unlaced
and the sole
    ah the soul
      a curious conception
   hanging on somehow
     to walk again
       in the free air
    once the heel
      has been replaced

SHORT STORY ON A PAINTING OF
GUSTAV KLIMT

They are kneeling upright on a flowered bed
He
    has just caught her there
              and holds her still
  Her gown
      has slipped down
           off her shoulder
He has an urgent hunger
      His dark head
         bends to hers
           hungrily
And the woman the woman
  turns her tangerine lips from his
    one hand like the head of a dead swan
    draped down over
             his heavy neck
      the fingers
        strangely crimped
          tightly together
  her other arm doubled up
        against her tight breast
  her hand a languid claw
        clutching his hand
  which would turn her mouth
           to his
  her long dress made
       of multicolored blossoms
       quilted on gold
  her Titian hair
    with blue stars in it
And his gold
    harlequin robe
      checkered with
        dark squares

Gold garlands
        stream down over
               her bare calves &
               tensed feet
Nearby there must be
        a jeweled tree
           with glass leaves aglitter
             in the gold air
It must be
        morning
           in a faraway place somewhere
They
   are silent together
              as in a flowered field
     upon the summer couch
             which must be hers
  And he holds her still
            so passionately
     holds her head to his
            so gently so insistently
     to make her turn
            her lips to his
Her eyes are closed
           like folded petals
She
   will not open
        He
          is not the One

A VAST CONFUSION

Long long I lay in the sands

Sound of trains in the surf
            in subways of the sea
And an even greater undersound
              of a vast confusion in the universe
     a rumbling and a roaring
                as of some enormous creature turning
                   under sea & earth
     a billion sotto voices murmuring
            a vast muttering
             a swelling stuttering
    in ocean's speakers
world's voice-box heard with ear to sand
               a shocked echoing
                 a shocking shouting
    of all life's voices lost in night
And the tape of it
              somehow running backwards now
through the Moog Synthesizer of time
                  Chaos unscrambled
                      back to the first
                        harmonies

And the first light

OLBERS' PARADOX

And I heard the learned astronomer
                whose name was Heinrich Olbers
        speaking to us across the centuries
        about how he observed with naked eye
            how in the sky there were
                    some few stars close up
        and the further away he looked
                the more of them there were
        with infinite numbers of clusters of stars
            in myriad Milky Ways & myriad nebulae

So that from this we may deduce
        that in the infinite distances
                    there must be a place
                    there *must* be a place
                    where all is light
    and that the light from that high place
                    where all is light
            simply hasn't got here yet
            which is why we still have night

But when at last that light arrives
        when at last it does get here
            the part of day we now call Night
            will have a white sky
                    with little black dots in it
                    little black holes
                        where once were stars
And then in that symbolic
            so poetic place
                    which will be ours
    we'll be our own true shadows
            and our own illumination
                        on a sunset earth

UPON REFLECTION

Night's black mirror is broken

the star crab has scuttled away

with the inkwell

into India

Dawn

sows its mustard seed

In the steep ravines and gulches

of Big Sur

small animals stir

under the tough underbrush

as sun creeps down the canyon walls

into the narrow meadows

where the wild quail

run & cluck

Daytime moon

after much reflection says

Sun is God

And the stream

standing still

rushes forward

DEEP CHESS

Life itself like championship chess
                              dark players jousting
                 on a checkered field
                              where you have only
                 so much time
                              to complete your moves
And your clock running
                              all the time
           and if you take
                      too much time
                                   for one move
              you have that much less
                                   for the rest
                   of your life
And your opponent
                      dark or fair
              (which may or may not be
                                   life itself)
bugging you with his deep eyes
   or obscenely wiggling his crazy eyebrows
      or blowing smoke in your face
         or crossing and recrossing his legs
                                   or her legs
or otherwise screwing around
   and acting like some insolent invulnerable
                              unbeatable god
       who can read your mind & heart
And one hasty move
                      may ruin you
         for you must play
                      deep chess
              (like the one deep game Spassky won from Fischer)
And if your unstudied opening
                              was not too brilliant
         you must play to win not draw

and suddenly come up with
                                a new Nabokov variation
And then lay Him out at last
                with some super end-game
                                no one has ever even dreamed of

And there's still time—
                                Your move

A RIVER STILL TO BE FOUND

Stoned &

singing Indian scat

with Ravi Shankar

(as if we knew him)

his sitar like a boat

by the 'river of life'

that flows on & on

into 'eternity'

Time itself a boat

upon that river

Slow distant figures

drawing barges

along those banks

the small drum a pulse

beating slow

under the skin

And our bodies

still in time—

transported—

dreamt eternal

by the Ganges—

a river

still to be found

in the interior

of America

THE GENERAL SONG OF HUMANITY

On the coast of Chile where Neruda lived
　　it's well known that
　　　　seabirds often steal
　　　　　　letters out of mailboxes
　　　　　　　which they would like to scan
　　　　　　　　for various reasons
Shall I enumerate the reasons?
　　They are quite clear
　　　　even given the silence of birds
　　　　　　　　　on the subject
　　　　(except when they speak of it
　　　　　　among themselves
　　　　　　　between cries)
First of all
　　they steal the letters because
　　　　they sense that the General Song
　　　　　　of the words of everyone
　　　　hidden in these letters
must certainly bear the keys
　　to the heart itself of humanity
　　　　which the birds themselves
　　　　　have never been able to fathom
　　(in fact entertaining much doubt
　　　that there actually are
　　　　　　hearts in humans)
And then these birds have a further feeling
　　that their own general song
　　　　might somehow be enriched
　　　　　by these strange cries of humans
　　(What a weird bird-brain idea
　　　that our titterings might enlighten them)
But when they stole away
　　　　with Neruda's own letters
　　　　　out of his mailbox at Isla Negra
　　　they were in fact stealing back

                    their own Canto General
          which he had originally gathered
                              from them
          with their omnivorous & ecstatic
                              sweeping vision
     But now that Neruda is dead
          no more such letters are written
          and they must play it by ear again—
               the high great song
                         in the heart of our blood & silence

Cuernavaca, October 26, '75

POPULIST MANIFESTO

Poets, come out of your closets,
Open your windows, open your doors,
You have been holed-up too long
in your closed worlds.
Come down, come down
from your Russian Hills and Telegraph Hills,
your Beacon Hills and your Chapel Hills,
your Mount Analogues and Montparnasses,
down from your foot hills and mountains,
out of your tepees and domes.
The trees are still falling
and we'll to the woods no more.
No time now for sitting in them
As man burns down his own house
to roast his pig.
No more chanting Hare Krishna
while Rome burns.
San Francisco's burning,
Mayakovsky's Moscow's burning
the fossil-fuels of life.
Night & the Horse approaches
eating light, heat & power,
and the clouds have trousers.
No time now for the artist to hide
above, beyond, behind the scenes,
indifferent, paring his fingernails,
refining himself out of existence.
No time now for our little literary games,
no time now for our paranoias & hypochondrias,
no time now for fear & loathing,
time now only for light & love.
We have seen the best minds of our generation
destroyed by boredom at poetry readings.
Poetry isn't a secret society,
It isn't a temple either.

Secret words & chants won't do any longer.
The hour of *om*ing is over,
the time for keening come,
time for keening & rejoicing
over the coming end
of industrial civilization
which is bad for earth & Man.
Time now to face outward
in the full lotus position
with eyes wide open,
Time now to open your mouths
with a new open speech,
time now to communicate with all sentient beings,
All you 'Poets of the Cities'
hung in museums, including myself,
All you poet's poets writing poetry about poetry,
All you dead language poets and deconstructionists,
All you poetry workshop poets
in the boondock heart of America,
All you house-broken Ezra Pounds,
All you far-out freaked-out cut-up poets,
All you pre-stressed Concrete poets,
All you cunnilingual poets,
All you pay-toilet poets groaning with graffitti,
All you A-train swingers who never swing on birches,
All you masters of the sawmill haiku
in the Siberias of America,
All you eyeless unrealists,
All you self-occulting supersurrealists,
All you bedroom visionaries
and closet agitpropagators,
All you Groucho Marxist poets
and leisure-class Comrades
who lie around all day
and talk about the workingclass proletariat,
All you Catholic anarchists of poetry,
All you Black Mountaineers of poetry,
All you Boston Brahmins and Bolinas bucolics,

All you den mothers of poetry,
All you zen brothers of poetry,
All you suicide lovers of poetry,
All you hairy professors of poesie,
All you poetry reviewers
drinking the blood of the poet,
All you Poetry Police—
Where are Whitman's wild children,
where the great voices speaking out
with a sense of sweetness and sublimity,
where the great new vision,
the great world-view,
the high prophetic song
of the immense earth
and all that sings in it
And our relation to it—
Poets, descend
to the street of the world once more
And open your minds & eyes
with the old visual delight,
Clear your throat and speak up,
Poetry is dead, long live poetry
with terrible eyes and buffalo strength.
Don't wait for the Revolution
or it'll happen without you,
Stop mumbling and speak out
with a new wide-open poetry
with a new commonsensual 'public surface'
with other subjective levels
or other subversive levels,
a tuning fork in the inner ear
to strike below the surface.
Of your own sweet Self still sing
yet utter 'the word en-masse'—
Poetry the common carrier
for the transportation of the public
to higher places
than other wheels can carry it.

Poetry still falls from the skies
into our streets still open.
They haven't put up the barricades, yet,
the streets still alive with faces,
lovely men & women still walking there,
still lovely creatures everywhere,
in the eyes of all the secret of all
still buried there,
Whitman's wild children still sleeping there,
Awake and sing in the open air.

THE OLD SAILORS

On the green riverbank
                                age late fifties
I am beginning
                        to remind myself
of my great Uncle Désir
                                in the Virgin Islands
On a Saint Thomas back beach
he lived when I last saw him
in a small shack
                        under the palms
Eighty years old
                                straight as a Viking
  (where the Danes once landed)
he stood looking out
                                over the flat sea
  blue eyes or grey
                                with the sea in them
salt upon his lashes
                        We
                were always sea wanderers
No salt here now
                        by the great river
        in the high desert range
Old sailors stranded
                the steelhead
                        they too lost without it
                                        leap up and die

WILD LIFE CAMEO, EARLY MORN

By the great river Deschutes
            on the meadowbank greensward
    sun just hitting
                the high bluffs
        stone cliffs sculpted
                        high away
            across the river

At the foot of a steep brown slope
                    a mile away
        six white-tail deer
    four young bucks with branched antlers
        and two small does
                        mute in eternity
                            drinking the river
    then in real time raising heads
        and climbing up and up
                    a steep faint switchback
            into full sun

I bring them close in the binoculars
                    as in a round cameo
    There is a hollow hole in a tree
                        one looks into
        One by one they
                    drink silence
        one by one
                climb up so calm
                    over the rim of the canyon
        and without looking back
                        disappear forever

Like certain people
            in my life

READING APOLLINAIRE BY
THE ROGUE RIVER

Reading Apollinaire here
sitting crosslegged
on sleepingbag & poncho
in the shadow of a huge hill
before the sun clears it
Woke up early on the shore
and heard the river shushing
(like the sound a snake might make
sliding over riprap
if you magnified the sound)
My head still down upon the ground
one eye without perspective
sees the stream sliding by
through the sand
as in a desert landscape
Like a huge green watersnake
with white water markings
the river slithers by
and where the canyon turns
and the river drops from sight
seems like a snake about to disappear
down a deep hole
Indians made their myths
of this great watersnake
slid down from mountains far away
And I see the Rogue for real
as the Indians saw him
the Rogue all wild white water
a cold-blooded creature
drowning and dousing
the Rogue ruler of the land
transforming it at will
with a will of its own
a creature to be feared and respected

pillaging its way to the sea
still ruled by that gravity
which still rules all
so that we might almost say
Gravity is God
manifesting Himself
as Great God Sun
who will one day make Himself
into a black hole in space
who will one day implode Himself
into Nothing
All of which the slithering Rogue
knows nothing of
in its headlong
blind rush to the sea
And though its head
is already being eaten
by that most cruel and churning
monster Ocean
the tail of the snake
knows it not
and continues turning & turning
toward its final hole
and toward that final black hole
into which all some day
will be sucked burning

As I sit reading a French poet
   whose most famous poem is about
      the river that runs through the city
         taking time & life & lovers with it
      And none returning
               none returning

ROUGH SONG OF ANIMALS DYING

In a dream within a dream I dreamt a dream
of the reality of existence
inside the ultimate computer
which is the universe
in which the Arrow of Time
flies both ways
through bent space
In a dream within a dream I dreamt a dream
of all the animals dying
the wild animals the longhaired animals
winged animals feathered animals
clawed & scaled & furry animals
rutting & dying & dying
In a dream within a dream I dreamt a dream
of creatures everywhere dying out
in shrinking rainforests
in piney woods & high sierras
on shrinking prairies & tumbleweed mesas
captured beaten strapped starved & stunned
cornered & traded
species not meant to be nomadic
wandering rootless as man
In a dream within a dream I dreamt a dream
of all the animals crying out
in their hidden places
slinking away & crawling about
through the last wild places
through the dense underbrush
the last Great Thickets
beyond the mountains
crisscrossed with switchbacks
beyond the marshes
beyond the plains & fences
(the West won with barbed-wire machines)
in the high country

in the low country
crisscrossed with highways
In a dream within a dream I dreamt a dream
of how they feed & rut & run & hide
In a dream within a dream I saw
how the seals are beaten on the ice-fields
the soft white furry seals with eggshell skulls
the Great Green turtles beaten & eaten
exotic birds netted & caged & tethered
rare wild beasts & strange reptiles & weird woozoos
hunted down for zoos
by bearded blackmarketeers
who afterwards ride around Singapore
in German limousines
In a dream within a dream I dreamt a dream
of the earth heating up & drying out
under its canopy of carbon dioxide
breathed out by a billion
infernal combustion engines
mixed with the sweet smell of burning flesh
In a dream within a dream I dreamt a dream
of animals calling to each other
in codes we never understand
The seal and steer cry out
in the same voice
as they are clubbed
in stockyards & snowfields
The wounds never heal
in the commonweal of animals
We steal their lives
to feed our own
and with their lives
our dreams are sown
In a dream within a dream I dreamt a dream
of the daily scrimmage for existence
in the wind-up model of the universe
the spinning meat-wheel world
in which I was a fish who eats his tail

in which I was a claw upon a beach
in which I was a snake upon a tree
in which I was a serpent's egg
a yin-yang yolk of good and evil
about to consume itself

HILARIOUS GOD

10 August '77 . . . Raft trip today / Up early to ride in a truck upriver to the starting point / The drought has reduced the size of the river by half / but still plenty of water / with rapids and deep pools full of sharp boulders and whirling funnels of white water / Too much sun, more than 100F out on the river / We shoot the first rapids in the rubber raft, get hung up between boulders in the middle of a riffle, lose an oar, get loose and recover it / And on down, as on a rollercoaster, laughing & shouting, some hilarious god in charge of us. . . . *11 August '77* . . . We are lost by the river / in stone solitude / only the sound of the river / to save us / from total stillness / from the total void / even the water only earth's breath / Nothing happening / nothing stirring / as if life itself had yet to begin / or were all over forever / Nirvana—or Samsara—or only the total boredom of the boondocks / We are saved / by a big recreational vehicle camper / that backs down the beach road / and parks almost on top of us / ladies in plastic haircurlers and little fuckers bearing plastic pails / bursting from it / screeching to the beach. *13 August '77 Siskiyou National Forest* . . . I put on the diving mask and went down / A few feet below the surface a few minnows circled me / A little further down a few small trout no more than three inches / I lie motionless just below the surface and search the deepest part of the pool / There at the very bottom between boulders / in the very deepest hole / I suddenly spy him / a huge fat grey speckled trout / perhaps eight pounds / perfectly still against the grey rocks / He would have been invisible from the surface / and invisible without the mask / Then suddenly I saw another fat speckled trout / not quite as big / quite close to the first / almost like his shadow / this one too perfectly motionless / as if not even breathing / though the swift stream poured by above it / Summer of the great drought / and this the only deep pool left / in this part of what had been a small river / now most of the streambed exposed / fifty feet of boulders and small rocks and gravel / the stream itself shrunk to a width of twenty feet / The pool isolated by rapids at each end / no more than two inches of water going over at any one spot / Last season the two fish must have made it up this far / then the stream shrunk still more / and here they were caught / in the shrinking hole / now no more than eight feet deep / where they lay motionless / waiting / trapped

/ their world shrinking and shrinking / Still they lie at the bottom / very still / conserving what they've got / They are fat from feeding on all the other dammed-up stream life around them / periwinkles / tiny minnows / crawdads and bugs / skeeters and tiny transparent wigglers that look like floating questionmarks / They are full and don't bite at anything / don't go for lures worms salmoneggs or bread / Fishermen don't have divingmasks and never see them down there and pass on quickly / as we dive down again & again / and see the fish in their steady-state of meditation / a final yoga discipline / which could go on until there is no water at all left in the stream / Then we might find them / still in swimming position / fins extended / mouth slightly open / eyes half closed / Or still later we might find their skeletons intact / in the same positions / baked in the firey sun / like Buddhist monks burned alive in lotus positions / Or still much later another age might discover / two fossil skeletons / imprinted on the boulders / at the very bottom of the crypt / as evidence of some former strange form / of a thing called Life / And if we stayed on here with them / waiting waiting / that later age / might also not be able to imagine one boy and his father fishing / by this stream / though our two round skulls be found / with the fishes / Yet seeing now the beauty of those fish / down there below the surface / so still and lovely / in their deep dream / dappled in their last deep pool / We fish no longer / turn / and go on / into the deeper pools / of our own lives.

THE OLD ITALIANS DYING

For years the old Italians have been dying
all over America
For years the old Italians in faded felt hats
have been sunning themselves and dying
You have seen them on the benches
in the park in Washington Square
the old Italians in their black high button shoes
the old men in their old felt fedoras
                                 with stained hatbands
have been dying and dying
                               day by day
You have seen them
every day in Washington Square San Francisco
the slow bell
tolls in the morning
in the Church of Peter & Paul
in the marzipan church on the plaza
toward ten in the morning the slow bell tolls
in the towers of Peter & Paul
and the old men who are still alive
sit sunning themselves in a row
on the wood benches in the park
and watch the processions in and out
funerals in the morning
weddings in the afternoon
slow bell in the morning Fast bell at noon
In one door out the other
the old men sit there in their hats
and watch the coming & going
You have seen them

the ones who feed the pigeons
                 cutting the stale bread
                         with their thumbs & penknives
the ones with old pocketwatches
the old ones with gnarled hands
                      and wild eyebrows
the ones with the baggy pants
                    with both belt & suspenders
the grappa drinkers with teeth like corn
the Piemontesi the Genovesi the Siciliani
                smelling of garlic & pepperoni
the ones who loved Mussolini
the old fascists
the ones who loved Garibaldi
the old anarchists reading *L'Umanita Nuova*
the ones who loved Sacco & Vanzetti
They are almost all gone now
They are sitting and waiting their turn
and sunning themselves in front of the church
over the doors of which is inscribed
a phrase which would seem to be unfinished
from Dante's *Paradiso*
about the glory of the One
                   who moves everything . . .
The old men are waiting
for it to be finished
for their glorious sentence on earth
                    to be finished
the slow bell tolls & tolls
the pigeons strut about
not even thinking of flying
the air too heavy with heavy tolling
The black hired hearses draw up
the black limousines with black windowshades
shielding the widows
the widows with the long black veils
who will outlive them all
You have seen them

madre di terra, madre di mare
The widows climb out of the limousines
The family mourners step out in stiff suits
The widows walk so slowly
up the steps of the cathedral
fishnet veils drawn down
leaning hard on darkcloth arms
Their faces do not fall apart
They are merely drawn apart
They are still the matriarchs
outliving everyone
the old dagos dying out
in Little Italys all over America
the old dead dagos
hauled out in the morning sun
that does not mourn for anyone
One by one Year by year
they are carried out
The bell
never stops tolling
The old Italians with lapstrake faces
are hauled out of the hearses
by the paid pallbearers
in mafioso mourning coats & dark glasses
The old dead men are hauled out
in their black coffins like small skiffs
They enter the true church
for the first time in many years
in these carved black boats
          ready to be ferried over
The priests scurry about
         as if to cast off the lines
The other old men
            still alive on the benches
watch it all with their hats on
You have seen them sitting there
waiting for the bocce ball to stop rolling
waiting for the bell

to stop tolling & tolling
for the slow bell
to be finished tolling
telling the unfinished *Paradiso* story
as seen in an unfinished phrase
on the face of a church
as seen in a fisherman's face
in a black boat without sails
making his final haul

THE SEA AND OURSELVES
AT CAPE ANN

Caw Caw Caw
on a far shingle long ago
when as a boy I came here
put ear to shell
           of the thundering sea
                    sundering sea
       seagulls high over
              calling & calling
         back then
           at Cape Ann Gloucester
Where Olson saw himself Ishmael
   and wrote his own epitaph:
            'I set out now
            in a box upon the sea'
And Creeley found his creel
      yet would not / cd. not
          speak of the sea
And Ferrini took the wind's clothes
      and became the conscience of Gloucester
Yet none could breathe
         a soul into the sea
And I saw the tide pools gasping
   the sea's mouth roaring
         polyphoboistrous
   beyond the Ten Pound Light
       roistering
         off far islands
   'Les Trois Sauvages'
Where Eliot heard
       the sea's stark meditation
  off *beauport* Gloucester
Where I as a man much later
      made a landfall in the gloaming

sighting from seaward in convoy
                    beyond the gulls' far off
                              tattered cries
          cats' cries lost
              reached to us
                    in shredded snatches
          Then as now
Eliot must
          have been a seaman
                    in his city-soul
     to have heard so deeply
               the sea's voice sounding then
                    in 'The Dry Salvages'
Here now
          where now
                    is the sea's urge still
     sea's surge and thunder
                         except within us
                    folded under
     by the beach road now
                         rapt in darkness
The sea still a great door never opened
          great ships asunder
                    clinker-built bottoms
               nets hung with cork
                    hulls heavy with caulking
While still the Nor'easter blows
               still the high tides
                    seethe & sweep shoreward
     batter the breakwaters
               the granite harbors
                         rock villages
          Land's End lashed again
                    in 'the sudden fury'
And still the stoned gulls soaring over
               crying & calling & crying
          blissed-out up there

                    in the darkening air
        over the running sea
                    the running sea
        over dark stone beach under stars
Where now we sit
                'distracted from distraction' still
        in parked cars

THE LOVE NUT

I go into the men's room Springfield bus station
on the way back to Muhlenberg County
and see this nut in the mirror
Who let in this weirdo Who let in this creep?
He's the kind writes I LOVE YOU on toilet walls and wants to
    embrace everybody in the lobby He writes his phone number
    inside a heart on the wall He's some kinda pervert Mister
    Eros the Great Lover
He wants to run up to everybody in the waiting room and kiss
    them on the spot and say Why aren't we friends and lovers
    Can I go home with you You got anything to drink or smoke
    Let's you and me get together The time is now or sooner
He wants to take all the stray dogs and cats and people home
    with him and turn them on to making love all the time
    wherever
He wants to scatter poems from airplanes across the landscape
    He's some kinda poetic nut Like he thinks he's Dylan
    Thomas and Bob Dylan rolled together with Charlie Chap-
    lin thrown in
He wants to lip-read everybody's thoughts and feelings and
    longings He's a dangerous nut He's gotta be insane He has
    no sense of sin
He wants to heat up all the dead-looking people the unhappy-
    looking people in bus stations and airports He wants to heat
    up their beds He wants to open their bodies and heads
He's some kinda airhead rolling stone He don't wanna be alone
    He may be queer on men
He's the kind addresses everybody on buses making them laugh
    and look away and then look back again
He wants to get everyone to burst out laughing and sighing and
    crying and singing and dancing and kissing each other in-
    cluding old ladies and policemen
He's gotta be mad He's so glad to be alive he's real strange He's
    got the hots for humanity one at a time He wants to kiss

your breasts He wants to lie still between them singing in a low voice

He wants everyone to lie down together and roll around together moaning and singing and having visions and orgasms He wants to come in you He wants you to come with him He wants us all to come together One hot world One heartbeat

He wants he wants us all to lie down together in Paradise in the Garden of Love in the Garden of Delights and couple together like a train a chain-reaction a chain-letter-of-love around the world on hot nights

He wants he wants he wants! He's gotta be crazy Call the cops Take him away!

TWO SCAVENGERS IN A TRUCK, TWO BEAUTIFUL PEOPLE IN A MERCEDES

At the stoplight waiting for the light
                      Nine A.M. downtown San Francisco
   a bright yellow garbage truck
           with two garbagemen in red plastic blazers
   standing on the back stoop
               one on each side hanging on
    and looking down into
               an elegant open Mercedes
     with an elegant couple in it
The man
      in a hip three-piece linen suit
        with shoulder-length blond hair & sunglasses
The young blond woman so casually coifed
          with a short skirt and colored stockings
    on the way to his architect's office

And the two scavengers up since Four A.M.
                  grungy from their route
       on the way home
The older of the two with grey iron hair
           and hunched back
     looking down like some
              gargoyle Quasimodo
And the younger of the two
           also with sunglasses & longhair
    about the same age as the Mercedes driver

And both scavengers gazing down
                as from a great distance
      at the cool couple
    as if they were watching some odorless TV ad
         in which everything is always possible

And the very red light for an instant
           holding all four close together
     as if anything at all were possible
                 between them
    across that small gulf
            in the high seas
                    of this democracy

HOME HOME HOME

Where are they going
all these brave intrepid animals
Fur and flesh
in steel cabinets
on wheels
high-tailing it
Four PM Friday freeway
over the hidden land
San Francisco's burning
with the late sun
in a million windows
The four-wheeled animals
are leaving it to burn
They're escaping
almost flying
home to the nest
home to the warm caves
in the hidden hills & valleys
home to daddy home to mama
home to the little wonders
home to the pot plants behind the garage
The cars the painted cabinets
streak for home home home
THRU TRAFFIC MERGE LEFT
home to the hidden turning
the hidden yearning
home to San Jose
home to Santa Cruz & Monterey
home to Hamilton Avenue
home to the Safeway the safest way
YIELD
LEFT LANE MUST TURN LEFT
home to the little grey home in the West
home to Granddaddy on the golfcourse
home to Uncle Ned

puttering in the toolshed
having lost his pants
on the stock exchange
home to big sister
who lost her way in encounter groups
home to the 97-lb housewife
driving two tons of chrome & steel
three blocks to the supermarket
to buy a package of baby pins
home to little sister
blushing with boyfriends
in the laundryroom
home to kid brother with skateboards & Adidas
home to mad Uncle building CB radios
in hidden bunkers
home to backyard barbecues
with aerospace neighbors
Mr. Wilson's coming over
The Hendersons will all be there
Home to Hidden Valley
where the widow waits
by the Cross on the mountain
where hangs the true madness
home to Santa's Village
WILL DIVIDE TO SUIT
GAS FOOD LODGING NEXT RIGHT
home to where the food is
home to Watsonville
home to Salinas
past the Grapes of Wrath
past United Farmworkers
stooped over artichokes
home home over the horizon
where the sun still blows
into the sea
home to Big Sur
and the oranges of Hieronymous Bosch
the sun still sets

in lavender skies
Home sweet home the salesman sighs
home safe at home in the bathroom
safe with the washingmachine & dishwasher
safe with the waterheater
safe with the kitchen clock
tick tick
the time is not yet
the alarm is set
safe at last in the double bed
hidden from each other
in the dark bed by the winding stair
the enchanted place in the still air
hidden each from each
or the queensize bed the kingsize bed
the waterbed with the vibrator
with the nylon nympho in it
the bed of roses
the bed with Big Emma in it
with the stoned-out Angel in it
(Mountains of flesh
Hills of hips & thighs
Rolling landscapes of heaving meat
Groans & moans & cries!)
Home to the bed we made
and must lie in
with 'whoever'
Or home to the bed still to be made
of ragas & visions
the bed whose form is pure light
(and unheard melodies
dark despairs & ecstasies
longings out of reach)
Who to decipher them who answer them
singing each to each?
Hidden from themselves
The beds are warm with them
The springs quake

on the San Andreas Fault
The dark land broods
Look in my eye, look in my eye
the cyclope tv cries
It blinks and rolls its glassy eye
and shakes its vacuum head
over the shaken bodies
in the bed

SAN JOSE SYMPHONY RECEPTION
(*Flagrante delicto*)

The bald man in plaid playing the harpsichord
    stopped short and sidled over
                        to the sideboard
      and copped a piece of Moka
                  on a silver plate
    and slid back and started playing again
        some kind of Hungarian rhapsodate
    while the lady with the green eyeshades
        leaned over him exuding
                    admiration & lust
Half notes danced & tumbled
                  out of his instrument
    exuding a faint odor of
              chocolate cake
In the corner I was taking
          a course in musical destruction
  from the dark lady cellist
    who bent over me with her bow unsheathed
    and proceeded to saw me in half
As a consequence my pants fell right off
    revealing a badly bent trombone which
      even the first flutist
        who had perfect embouchure
            couldn't straighten out

AN ELEGY TO DISPEL GLOOM

(After the assassinations of Mayor George Moscone and Supervisor Harvey Milk in San Francisco, November, 1978)

Let us not sit upon the ground
and tell sad stories
of the death of sanity.
Two humans made of flesh
are meshed in death
and no more need be said.
It is pure vanity
to think that all humanity
be bathed in red
because one young mad man
one so bad man
lost his head.
The force that through the red fuze
drove the bullet
does not drive everyone
through the City of Saint Francis
where there's a breathless hush
in the air today
a hush at City Hall
and a hush at the Hall of Justice
a hush in Saint Francis Wood
where no bird
tries to sing
a hush on the Great Highway
and in the great harbor
upon the great ships
and on the Embarcadero
from the Mission Rock Resort
to the Eagle Cafe
a hush on the great red bridge
and on the great grey bridge
a hush in the Outer Mission
and at Hunter's Point

a hush at a hot potato stand on Pier 39
and a hush at the People's Temple
where no bird
tries its wings
a hush and a weeping
at the Convent of the Sacred Heart
on Upper Broadway
a hush upon the fleshpots
of Lower Broadway
a pall upon the punk rock
at Mabuhay Gardens
and upon the cafes and bookstores
of old North Beach
a hush upon the landscape
of the still wild West
where two sweet dudes are dead
and no more need be said.
Do not sit upon the ground and speak
of other senseless murderings
or worse disasters waiting
in the wings.
Do not sit upon the ground and talk
of the death of things beyond
these sad sad happenings.
Such men as these do rise above
our worst imaginings.

ADIEU À CHARLOT
(*Second Populist Manifesto*)

Sons of Whitman sons of Poe
sons of Lorca & Rimbaud
or their dark daughters
poets of another breath
poets of another vision
Who among you still speaks of revolution
Who among you still unscrews
the locks from the doors
in this revisionist decade?
'You are President of your own body, America'
Thus spoke Kush in Tepotzlan
youngblood wildhaired angel poet
one of a spawn of wild poets
in the image of Allen Ginsberg
wandering the wilds of America
'You Rimbauds of another breath'
sang Kush
and wandered off with his own particular paranoias
maddened like most poets
for one mad reason or another
in the unmade bed of the world
Sons of Whitman
in your 'public solitude'
bound by blood-duende
'President of your own body America'
Take it back from those who have maddened you
back from those who stole it
and steal it daily
The subjective must take back the world
from the objective gorillas & guerrillas of the world
We must rejoin somehow
the animals in the fields
in their steady-state meditation
'Your life is in your own hands still

Make it flower make it sing'
(so sang mad Kush in Tepotzlan)
'a constitutional congress of the body'
still to be convened to seize control
of the State
the subjective state
from those who have subverted it
The arab telephone of the avant-garde
has broken down
And I speak to you now
from another country
Do not turn away
in your public solitudes
you poets of other visions
of the separate lonesome visions
untamed uncornered visions
fierce recalcitrant visions
you Whitmans of another breath
which is not the too-cool breath of modern poetry
which is not the halitosis of industrial civilization
Listen now Listen again
to the song in the blood the dark duende a dark singing
between the tickings of civilization
between the lines of its headlines
in the silences between cars
driven like weapons
In two hundred years of freedom
we have invented
the permanent alienation of the subjective
almost every truly creative being
alienated & expatriated
in his own country
in Middle America or San Francisco
the death of the dream in your birth
o meltingpot America
I speak to you
from another country
another kind of blood-letting land

from Tepotzlan the poets' lan'
Land of the Lord of the Dawn
                                  Quetzalcoatl
Land of the Plumed Serpent
I signal to you
as Artaud signaled
through the flames
I signal to you
over the heads of the land
the hard heads that stand like menhirs
above the land in every country
the short-haired hyenas
who still rule everything
I signal to you from Poets' Land
you poets of the alienated breath
to take back your land again
and the deep sea of the subjective
Have you heard the sound of the ocean lately
the sound by which daily
the stars still are driven
the sound by which nightly
the stars retake their sky
The sea thunders still to remind you
of the thunder in the blood
to remind you of your selves
Think now of your self
as of a distant ship
Think now of your beloved
of the eyes of your beloved
whoever is most beloved
he who held you hard in the dark
or she who washed her hair by the waterfall
whoever makes the heart pound
the blood pound
Listen says the river
Listen says the sea Within you
you with your private visions
of another reality a separate reality

Listen and study the charts of time
Read the sanskrit of ants in the sand
You Whitmans of another breath
there is no one else to tell
how the alienated generations
have lived out their expatriate visions
here and everywhere
The old generations have lived them out
Lived out the bohemian myth in Greenwich Villages
Lived out the Hemingway myth
in *The Sun Also Rises*
at the Dôme in Paris
or with the bulls at Pamplona
Lived out the Henry Miller myth
in the *Tropics* of Paris
and the great Greek dream
of *The Colossus of Maroussi*
and the tropic dream of Gauguin
Lived out the D. H. Lawrence myth
in *The Plumed Serpent*
in Mexico Lake Chapala
And the Malcolm Lowry myth
Under the Volcano at Cuernavaca
And then the saga of *On the Road*
and the Bob Dylan myth Blowing in the Wind
How many roads must a man walk down
How many Neal Cassadys on lost railroad tracks
How many replicas of Woody Guthrie with cracked guitars
How many photocopies of longhaired Joan
How many Ginsberg facsimiles and carbon-copy Keseys
still wandering the streets of America
in old tennis shoes and backpacks
or driving beat-up school buses
with destination-signs reading 'Further'
How many Buddhist Catholics how many cantors
chanting the Great Paramita Sutra
on the Lower East Side
How many Whole Earth Catalogs

lost in out-houses on New Mexico communes
How many Punk Rockers waving swastikas
Franco is dead but so is Picasso
Chaplin is dead but I'd wear his bowler
having outlived all our myths but his
the myth of the pure subjective
the collective subjective
the Little Man in each of us
waiting with Charlot or Pozzo
On every corner I see them
those lost subjective selves
hidden inside their tight clean clothes
Their hats are not derbys they have no canes
They turn and hitch their pants
and walk away from us
in the great American night

(Tepotzlan '75—San Francisco '78)

RETIRED BALLERINAS,
CENTRAL PARK WEST

Retired ballerinas on winter afternoons
            walking their dogs
                    in Central Park West
            (or their cats on leashes—
            the cats themselves old highwire artists)
The ballerinas
            leap and pirouette
                    through Columbus Circle
            while winos on park benches
                    (laid back like drunken Goudonovs)
            hear the taxis trumpet together
                    like horsemen of the apocalypse
                            in the dusk of the gods
It is the final witching hour
                    when swains are full of swan songs
And all return through the dark dusk
            to their bright cells
                    in glass highrises
            or sit down to oval cigarettes and cakes
                    in the Russian Tea Room
            or climb four flights to back rooms
                            in Westside brownstones
            where faded playbill photos
                    fall peeling from their frames
                    like last year's autumn leaves

ENDLESS LIFE

Endless the splendid life of the world
Endless its lovely living and breathing
its lovely sentient beings
seeing and hearing feeling and thinking
laughing and dancing sighing and crying
through endless afternoons endless nights
drinking and doping talking and singing
in endless Amsterdams of existence
with endless lively conversations
over endless cups of coffee
in literary cafes on rainy mornings
Endless street movies passing
in cars and trams of desire
on the endless tracks of light
And endless longhair dancing
to airless punk rock and airhead disco
through Milky Way midnights
to the Paradisos of dawn
talking and smoking and thinking
of everything endless at night
in the white of night the light of night
Ah yes oh yes the endless living and loving
hating and loving kissing and killing
Endless the ticking breathing breeding
meat-wheel of life
turning on and on through time
Endless life and endless death
endless air and endless breath
Endless worlds without end of days
in autumn capitals
their avenues of leaves ablaze
Endless dreams and sleep unravelling
the knitted sleeves of care
the labyrinths of thought
the labyrêves of love

the coils of desire and longing
myriad endgames of the unnameable
Endless the heavens on fire
endless universe spun out
World upon a mushroom pyre
Endless the fire that breathes in us
tattooed fire-eaters dancing in plazas
swallowing flaming gasoline air
Brave the beating heart of flaming life
its beating and pulsings and flame-outs
Endless the open fields of the senses
the smell of lust and love
the calling and calling of cats in heat
their scent of must of musk
No end to the sound of the making of love
to the sound of bed springs creaking
to the moan of lovers making it
heard through the wall at night
No end to their groans of ecstasy
moans of the last lost climax
the sound of jukebox jumping
the flow of jass and gyzm
jived in Paradiso
And then the endless attempts to escape
the *nausée* of Sartre
the bald hills of burned out sensation
joie de vivre in despair
boatloads of enlightenment
ships of *merde* afloat by Charon's moat
greeds hysterias paranoias
pollutions and perversions
Endless *l'homme revolté*
in the anonymous face of death
in the tracks of the monster state
Endless his anarchist visions
endless his alienation
endless his alienated poetry
gadfly of the state Bearer of Eros

Endless the sound of this life of man on earth
his endless radio broadcasts and tv transmissions
newspapers rolling off endless rolls on rotary presses
the flow of his words and images
on endless typewriter ribbons and tapes
automatic writings and scrawlings
endless *poèmes dictés* by the unknown
Endless the calling on telephones to ends of earth
the waiting of lovers on station platforms
the crying of birds on hills and rooftops
the cawing and cawing of crows in the sky
the myriad churming of crickets
the running seas the crying waters
rising and falling on far shingles
the lapping of tides
in the Ides of autumn
salt kiss of creation
No end to the sea bells tolling
beyond the dams and dykes of life
and the calling and calling of bells
in empty churches and towers of time
No end to the calamitous enunciation
of hairy holy man
Endless the ever-unwinding
watchspring heart of the world
shimmering in time
shining through space
Endless the tourist-boats through it
bateaux mouches in endless canals
millions of windows aflame in sunset
the City burns with leftover light
and red light districts rock and glow
with endless porn and neon cocks
and vibrators vibrating endlessly
in lonely topfloor rooms of leaning houses
Endless the munching
on the meat-sandwiches of lust
the juicy steaks of love

endless dreams and orgasms
fertility rites and rites of passage
and flights of fertile birds over rooftops
and the dropping of eggs in nests and wombs
the tempts and attempts of the flesh
in furnished rooms of love
where sings the stricken dove
No end to the birthing of babies
where love or lust has lain
no end to the sweet birth of consciousness
no end to the bitter deaths of it in vain
No end no end to the withering
of fur and fruit and flesh so passing fair
and the neon mermaids
singing each to each somewhere
Endless the slight variations
of the utterly familiar
the fires of youth the embers of age
the rage of the poet born again
No end no end to any and all creation
in the mute dance of molecules
All is transmuted All is muted
and all cries out again again
Endless the waiting for God and Godot
the absurd actions absurd plans and plays
dilemmas and delays
Absurd the waiting without action
for the withering away of war
and the withering away of the state
Insane the waiting without action
for the insane ending!
Endless the wars of good and evil
the flips of fate the trips of hate
endless nukes and faults all failing-safe
in endless chain reactions of the final flash
while the White Bicycles of protest
still slowly circle round it
For there will be an end to the dogfaced gods

in wingtip shoes in Gucci slippers
in Texas boots and tin hats
in bunkers pressing buttons
For there is no end to the hopeful choices
still to be chosen
the dark minds lighted
the green giants of chance
the fish-hooks of hope in the sloughs of despond
the hills in the distance the birds in the bush
hidden streams of light and unheard melodies
sessions of sweet silent thought
stately pleasure domes decreed
and the happy deaths of the heart every day
the cocks of clay
the feet in running shoes
upon the quai
And there is no end
to the doors of perception still to be opened
and the jet-streams of light
in the upper air of the spirit of man
in the outer space inside us
in the Amsterdams of yin & yang
Endless rubaiyats and endless beatitudes
endless shangri-las endless nirvanas
sutras and mantras
satoris and sensaras
Bodhiramas and Boddhisatvas
karmas and karmapas!
Endless singing Shivas dancing
on the smoking wombs of ecstasy!
Shining! Transcendent!
into the crystal night of time
in the endless silence of the soul
in the long loud tale of man
in his endless sound and fury
signifying everything
with his endless hallucinations
adorations annihilations illuminations

erections and exhibitions
fascismo and machismo
circuses of the soul astray
merrygorounds of the imagination
coney island of the mindless
endless poem dictated
by the uncollected voice
of the collective unconscious
blear upon the tracks of time!

In the last days of Alexandria
The day before Waterloo
The dancing continues
There is a sound of revelry by night

Amsterdam, July 1980

PARIS TRANSFORMATIONS

1.

Clay somnambule returned
                          after many years away
            walking and walking
                          through once-loved Paris
            Gare du Nord to Montparnasse
                Rue de la Roquette and Place Voltaire
                    Place Léon Blum and Père Lachaise
                        Les Halles and Tour St. Jacques
                            Saint Sulpice and Cherche Midi
                            (where I searched my Noon)

Strode through the streets
                    thirsty and sad
                                (yet exultant!)
                carrying nothing
                            but youth

Now the closed bus carries me
                        past the place I lay on the quai

The map of Paris
                    stamped upon my brainpan

2.

I left my memory in hock
on the rooftops of Paris
where the grey light of Paris lies

like the shadow at the back of old mirrors
And the sky a grey scrim behind the river
where at noon the sun bursts through
with a golden stroke,
a scimitar ablaze,
tearing the veil of days.

3.

That lovely balcony is gone
                    in the Impasse Danton
          and with it the lady
                    with the scales
          who sat there once
                    (the blind one in the classic frieze)
Now an ounce of memory
                    moves these scales in a breeze
I feel the weight of her breast
                    against me pressed

But she was young then
                    and wore no blindfold
          (Blind maiden
                    not blind in love!)
I hold her hand still
                    like a limp white glove

4.

In the closed dark bedroom
with the heavy silk drapes
she throws open
the huge French doors
And the dry white wine of dawn
floods in

5.

The white sun of Paris
softens sidewalks
sketches white shadows on skylights
traps a black cat
on a distant balcony

And the whole city sleeping drifts
through white space
like a lost dirigible
unconscious of
the immense mystery

6.

Place Saint Sulpice
                le soir
Lady in a coal-shovel hat
                        crosses the street
Dupré's organ music
                follows her from the church
A black poodle
                also follows her
                                like a shadow
The leaves of the plane trees quiver
                        as if expecting rain
A fat dame in a plain apron
                stands at the bar with a crutch
        at the back of the *Café de la Mairie*
                                du Sixième
                and eats a *Croque-Monsieur*
                with her
                                false teeth
                        her face
                                fallen out of Goya
A priest comes out and closes
                the iron gate of the church

Six minutes later he cycles past
        with flowers on the back
                of his old clunker
The dusk descends
The people all disappear
              into doorways
The sidewalks like flat escalators
          roll away into the night
Trees, fountains, statues,
         the café and the church itself
    melt into total darkness
As still somewhere
        a bell tolls
           the mad idea
    of a Christian society

7.

The big barges push through
under the Pont Mirabeau.
A huge sculptured mermaid
with golden torch
looks down upon them.
A barge man in black beret
looks up
the same way he looked up
at the last bridge
at the first Statue of Liberty
with eyes like worn pennies.

*Et sous le Pont Mirabeau
coule la liberté.*

8.

A homesick jade elephant
with eyes half-closed
sits by the Seine

in the lotus position
dreaming of the Nile

He puts his trunk in the river
and siphons up the sound
of October and autos
and the smell of distant spring
which is Paris echoing
some lost life
of wonder and laughter
in which Myrna Loy might appear
with Ramon Novarro singing to her
an Arabian Love Song
floating down the river
in a felucca

9.

He's walking about
in his Egyptian pajamas.
Through the side streets of Paris
the little narrow alleys
he's leading his humpy camel.
He has a halo on his head
which will not go away
as in Marcel Aymé.
The camel will not fit through
some of the crooked alleys.
It is like trying to pull him through
the eye of a rusty needle.
Also the halo gets stuck
in the low branches of trees.
Nevertheless he must cross Paris
with his camel and his halo.
Once in a while a sniper on a rooftop
takes a shot at him.
But the bullets bounce off his halo
like pinballs in a slot machine.

When they finally reach
the far end of town
they lie down together
the camel and the man with the halo
in the Egyptian pajamas.
But they cannot sleep or make love.
The camel's hump and the halo
always get in the way.
Suddenly they are seized
with uncontrollable laughter.
And they roll around together on the ground
convulsed with the thought
of their cosmic situation on earth.

10.

Tristes banlieues,
saisons, châteaux,
et toutes ces tristesses
de la Ligne de Sceaux.
But then again the things that still amaze
And autumn capitols
their avenues of leaves ablaze
avec leurs douces fugues,
tristes banlieues,
saisons, châteaux,
et toutes ses tristes joies
qui ont lieu
au coeur brisé.

11.

My hand was not mine
It wandered over my body all night
looking for a place to rest
Sartre's nausea filled my being
A chestnut branch
reached in the window

and scratched my heart
A tired cicada
started taking off its skin
Only the singing
of a distant swan
saved me from swooning away
A huge bumblebee flew in
and awarded me a golden sting
I fell over sideways
my tongue in a sling

12.

I meant to pick a paper poppy
from the fields of Normandy
the coquelicots of Monet
in my memory
and memory a mix of blooms
unpicked in rime
a mix of wings
untied in time
So that a coquelicot
becomes an orange sun
when day is
almost done
And the blind sphinx of life
eats my mind

13.

For years I never thought of death.
Now the breath
of the eternal harlequin
makes me look up
as if a defrocked Someone were there
who might make me into an angel
playing piano on a riverboat.

RETURNING TO PARIS WITH PISSARRO

I am in a painting by Camille Pissarro
Place du Théâtre Français
Paris in the Rain 1898
only it is not 1898
It is 1948
a slight juggling of numbers
and no horse carriages
but the same eternal feeling
sad and elated
walking in Paris in the rain
I can feel it coming through
the French canvas
the light rain falling
out of the pearl skies
the Opera a deep pearl
in the far distance
of the Avenue de l'Opéra
And the domed roofs of the Théâtre Français
the stricken winter trees
the smell of Gaulois at the Metro entrance
(which doesn't exist yet in the picture)
the fountain in front of the Théâtre
still spouting in the rain
And the dark chimneys
above the wet mansard roofs
above the fifth floor running balconies
and the grey awnings along the Avenue
dark figures under umbrellas
two by two
or clustered at corners
The grey Paris light
lies on the great buildings
like a light gauze veil
the lucent light
glimmers on the wet paving

on the sidewalks under the trees
You can almost hear
the clop-clop of horses
drawing the fiacres
The rain has let up
It seems about to clear
the veil to be torn away
pearl about to open
in the sky of 1948—
I am *twenty*-eight
with new eyes alight
returning to Paris with Pissarro
from the New World

French Impressionist painter Camille Pissarro (1830–1903) born St. Thomas, Virgin Islands

A DARK PORTRAIT

She always said *'tu'* in such a way

as if she wanted to sleep with you

or had just had

        a most passionate

                  orgasm

And she *tutoyé*d everyone

But she

      was really like Nora in *Nightwood*

long-gaited and restless as a mare

and coursed the cafés

        through revolving doors and nights

looking for the lover

        who would never satisfy her

And when she grew old

        slept among horses

CAFÉ NOTRE DAME

A sort of sexual trauma
has this couple in its thrall
He is holding both her hands
in both his hands
She is kissing his hands
They are looking
in each other's eyes
up close
She has a fur coat
made of a hundred running rabbits
He
is wearing a formal
dark coat and dove grey trousers
Now they are inspecting the palms
of each other's hands
as if they were maps of Paris
or of the world
as if they were looking for the Metro
that would take them together
through subterranean ways
through the stations of desire
to love's final terminals
at the ports of the city of light
It is a terminal case
But they are losing themselves
in the crisscrossing lines
of their intertwined palms
their head-lines and their heart-lines
their fate-lines and life-lines
illegibly entangled
in the *mons veneris*
of their passion

MAKING LOVE IN POETRY

(After André Breton)

In a war where every second counts
Time drops to the ground
like a shadow from a tree
under which we lie
in a wood boat built from it
by an unknown carpenter beyond the sea
upon which peach pits float
fired by a gunner who has run out of ammunition
for a cannon whose muzzle bites heartshaped holes
out of the horizon of our flesh
stunned in sun and baffled into silence
between the act of sex
and the act of poetry
at the moment of loving and coming
there is no glimpsing of
the misery of the world

VOIX GLAUQUE

Now that bird of life
                   with its *bouche avare*
      makes as if to devour us

Except it cannot do it
           as long as we keep singing
                        and making love
        for this sets up vibrations
                  in its throat
        which make it impossible
                 to swallow us

It is the dead bird
        in the heart
            that kills us

As on this Sunday afternoon
               sky grey over Les Halles
    from the fifth floor balcony
        I see stick figures lost below
               the mute singers and the walking dead
     And one pigeon walks about silent
        and one or two
              fly through the heavy air
It does not matter that the sky
              is made of lead
     or that no bells toll
           anywhere

Inside ourselves is the song
            as in an *oboe d'amore*
It sounds in us so distantly
             so insistently
      a distant singing
          a far crying

                    so faintly echoing—
                              glaucous voice
                         beyond our little turning world
          It is life itself singing
                    its exultant harmonies
               and stretching over us
                         its darkling wings

HE WITH THE BEATING WINGS

The lark has no tree
                    the crow no roost
        the owl no setting place
                    the nightingale
                                no certain song
    And he with the beating wings
                        no place to light
                                in the neon dawn
                his tongue too long ago
                                retuned
            by those ornithologists
                            the state has hired
            to make sure
                    the bird population of the world
                remains stable
                            and pinioned
    There is no need
                to clip its claws
    Its tongue will do
                Tether the tongue
        and all falls fallow
                The wild seed drops
                        into nothingness
    Tether the tongue
                and all falls
                            into silence
            a condition ever desired
                            by tyrants
                not least of which is
                                the great state
            with its benevolent birdwatchers
                            with their nets and binoculars
    watching out for
                the wild one
        He that bears Eros

                    like a fainting body
          He that bears
                         the gold bough
     He
        with the beating wings

L'OCCUPATION OBSÉDÉE

for Jacques Prévert

Assis sur la terrasse Café Saint-Séverin
J'entends des voix allemandes de chaque côté
Et la voix américaine
le Latin de nos jours
Avec son empire qui roule toujours
C'est toujours Normandie 1944
Avec ses voix américaines et ses voix allemandes
Suis toujours en train de débarquer!
Je lis toujours *Le Canard Enchainé*
Je lis *Libération* toujours
Je vois encore l'oiseau délabré
J'entends encore la voix criante
La voix palpitante
de l'accordéon
dans le métro
l'hiver 1944
Où je sens encore
les Gauloises Jaunes
Suis toujours occupé
occupé des rêves-pensées
Qui me disent que la vie toujours
est noble et tragique
et les barques d'amour toujours
se brisent sur les côtes
de la vie de tous-les-jours
de la vie hebdomadairienne
du *Monde Hebdomadaire*
où je lis encore
qu'il y a toujours la Résistance
qu'on va contrôler bien sur
Oui, la Résistance toujours
contre l'état monstre
contre les chaines sur l'oiseau
Ah lost gardens

Forgotten fountains
Tournesols détournés
Cannabis caché
L'herbe *sin semilla*
Oiseau frappé
bouche bouclée
Fraternité.

TRISTE CORBIÈRE

A clamor of gulls
outside the French windows
above the tidepools
in the stone harbor
in Roscoff Brittany
in the Hotel des Bains
top floor under the eaves
I look down and see
the damned poet
Tristan Corbière
walking along the quai
in this stone town
with its fishscale skies
where a street is named after him
a small dark stone street
twisting to the sea
Even at this distance
I see the black crow's feet
on his head
where a crow gripped him
and tried to fly away with him
Triste Corbière
with your countenance of night
Now a black gull
flies away with a fish
in the dark daylight
And a black crow watches
from a great height
an ebony crow
a huge crow
made of nothing but night
Only his feet are red
from holding the head of the poet
red with the blood of the poet
with his countenance of night

MORLAIX: INTO THE FUTURE
WITH NEIL YOUNG

At the Café de la Terrasse
I've given myself up
to the essence of things
trying to tune in on
what's going on here
if anything
Young French would-be punk-rock stars
listening to American westerns on the juke
trying to figure out
how to get out of town
Son of the local pork butcher
in leather pants and dark glasses
snaps his fingers to the beat
figuring out nothing
A slight wind has come up
with the smell of roast chestnuts
in this little town of Morlaix
with its stone aqueduct high-over
The town bandstand empty
The chestnut trees around it
waving their lush leaves
Nothing else moves It's the provinces
deep summer
Neil Young comes on the juke
You can almost see his Stetson
and the hole in his guitar
An old nag clops around a corner
into the Place de la Mairie
Suddenly following the horse
an amazing cavalcade appears
a troupe of masked mummers
to the sound of a flute and a small tambour
beaten with a stick
The mystery behind their masks

must remain a mystery
as if it were life itself
Otherwise these would-be escapees
might not run off with this travelling show of life
in their hot youth and heat
over the hill through time and dangers
to the crystal canyons
and the Motel of Lost Companions
with heated pool and waterbeds
full of shining strangers

PLAN DU CENTRE DE PARIS
À VOL D'OISEAU

Flying away to Milan
I look down and back at Paris
(as in that famous map
seen by a bird in flight)
and think of Allen yesterday
saying it was all 'solidified nostalgia'—
houses monuments and streets
bare trees and parks down there
fixed in time (and the time is forever)
exactly where we left them years ago
our bodies passed through them
as through a transparent scrim
Early versions of ourselves
transmuted now
two decades later
And was that myself
standing on that far corner
Place Saint-Sulpice
first arrived in Paris—
seabag slung—
(fancying myself some seaborn Conrad
carrying Coleridge's albatross?)
or was that myself walking
through the Tuileries in snow?
And here Danton met Robespierre
(both later to descend into earth
through that Metro entrance)
And here Sartre lived with Beauvoir
above the Café Bonaparte
before death
shook them apart
(The myth goes on)
And here in the Luxembourg
I sat by a balustrade

in a rented iron chair
reading Proust and Apollinaire
while the day turned to dust
and a nightwood sprang up around me
Solidified nostalgia indeed—
the smell of Gaulois still hangs in the air
And in the cemetery of Père Lachaise
the great stone tombs still yawn
with the solidified ennui of eternity
And, yes, here I knew such aloneness—
at the corner of another street
the dawn yawned
in some trauma I was living in back then
Paris itself a floating dream
a great stone ship adrift
made of dusk and dawn and darkness—
dumb trauma
of youth!
such wastes of love
such wordless hungers
mute neuroses
yearnings & gropings
fantasies & flame-outs
such endless walking
through the bent streets
such fumbling art
(models drawn with blindfolds)
such highs and sweet inebriations—
I salute you now
dumb inchoate youth
(callow stripling!)
and offer you my left hand
with a slight derisive laugh

FIRENZE, A LIFETIME LATER

'A cavatina of broken parlando utterances'
    punctuated by sighs
        was the sound of the river Arno passing through
        that Tuscan countryside that evening
          as we lay on a grass bank
            trailing our hands in the ochre waters
    as if we were students again
      just hitchhiked down from Paris
and as if this dreamt re-enactment
    might have the same ending again
      as that first time we
          returned to the same *pensione*
    and made love in the same *camera*
      to the dark tremolo of the same doves
Only this time
      our lives not shaken
            by our coming

THE LIGHT

Couples on the boat to the Isola di Giglio
in the Tuscan archipelago
wrapped up in each other
What does he see in her
and her in him—
He strokes her leg
She loves him
What a look
she lays on him
I love you
It's a mystery
It continues
There's an old *pescatore* watching them
He wishes he were him
Obviously he's come a long way
the fisher with his face like Sicily
with his hands like crabs
He would like to haul her in
but his net already has
too many fish in it
He's already hauled it in
too many times
with big old ones and little ones
stuck in the net
his *famiglia*
Still he eyes the Venus on the hook
as if it were his
as if he had caught it
and didn't quite know
what to do with it
It's the eternal mystery
Fat legs she has
but a face from a Greek coin
the light of Greece in it
Ah yes that's it

the light in the eyes
in spite of all
fat legs and dim brain
tuttavia
It's the light that counts
the light that attracts the fish at night

JOHN LENNON IN THE
PORTO SANTO STEFANO

A *trattoria* in the *porto:*
an astonishingly beautiful couple enters
in shorts
He's got a fantastic torso
long hair and a golden headband
She's got long flaxen hair
German hippies maybe
Bourgeois back home
Another couple saunters in and joins them
Dark hair and jeans
Comme ils sont beaux
Not one of them is gay
though he's the most beautiful
He's got such a smile
Some story he's telling
What could it be
Something about John Lennon
lost in a mix of Tuscan and German
Comme elle est belle
with her empty eyes
the Germans very spaced out
the Italians very "with it"
But none of them look very happy
Perhaps it's just youth
I am trying to think of a Lennon line
to sum up the situation
There isn't any
He didn't live long enough to give us
the mad eternal answer

THE MOUTH OF TRUTH

Is this the mouth of truth
in the face of this woman
walking across the *Piazza
Bocca della Verità*
where the great round stone is set up
in the portico of the Church of
Santa Maria in Cosmedin
her little feet taking her
past the Temple of the Virgins
past the Temple of the Phallus
and past the Street of the Misericordia
She has not been kneeling
in any church
She trots along on her too high heels
She has smart rhinestone glasses
and silk pants very well cut
She has a sweet face
spoiled by lipstick
a botched attempt
at something but the truth
She could be the daughter of a shah
but she isn't
She's some secretary
Late at the office
the boss was beastly tonight
Her mouth must have answered
Those rouge lips could cope with
any tongue
She's tough in a way
but not so tough
She has her soft spots
her lower lip
is very sensitive
You can tell there are other soft places

from that
She has her cigarette lit
in her right hand
the same hand she may have put
into the Mouth of Truth
that great round pagan stone
at the mouth of the church
which will bite off your hand
if you're hiding some lie
She did not put her head
into the mouth of the lion
Her left hand has rings
in the wrong places
She doesn't have a boyfriend
this year
but she has her cigarette
You can tell it is a close friend
the way she fondles it
It is a filter tip
She is looking forward
to lying down on her bed
in the dark
in her slip
with the window open
There is a tree outside
In the morning a bird
She is smoking her cigarette
her mouth of truth around the filter
which has filtered out
all but the truth
The truth will come through
the truth will out
the mouth fall open
when she's asleep on her back
by the open window
by the tree with its leaves like lips
the lower lip so sensitive

will quiver
the throat utter some deep sound
the tongue mute messenger
with its speechless truth
To whom will she tell it
in what dream. . . .

from **CANTI ROMANI**

IV

At midnight on the next balcony
a naked man standing in the dense dark
smoking and looking down
Across the way a naked lady unaware
comes out and sits upon a chair
They do not see each other
in the curtained air
At dawn they are gone
and thousands of swallows
flicker down
silent, flittering
flickering over the rooftops
It is as if the muted air
were made of the down of their wings
of the sound the hushed sound
of their wings
which none but another bird could hear
It is as if the first light
were made for singing
It is as if Dante were walking
from roof to roof
lightly singing
        a muted melody
lightly humming
         to himself
            a fretted threnody
lightly treading
        the tiled balconies
     the marble terraces
The swallows
        swirl about him
With the dawn they dart away
leaving feathers in his hair

woven like laurel
>   in the sweet air
>   so full of our strange life
>   so bitter yet so passing fair

V

Along the Appian Way
children are playing
imitating marching soldiers and battles
chattering and shrieking like swallows
>   at evening
There is a thrill in the air
a sound of tiny tin drums
hidden somewhere
>   over the hills
as if there were a fair somewhere
which we were not allowed to approach
a fair militaire
which retreats always beyond us
beyond the horizon
as we advance
waving our colored rags of flags
Furiously
we wave them
imitating marching soldiers and battles
Avànti!
Combàttere! Obbedire!
Lòtta Continua!
Lining the great Way
the crowds cheer
>   waving their ragged rainbows
The dusk is falling
the children disappear
babies rolled away in prams
crowds melted
>   into nothingness
Only the great pines remain

the great still trees
                  the heavy-headed trees
as in a Turner landscape
as a great silence descends
on the windless reaches
And then far away
far off and faint
intermittent
hesitant
heard and unheard
as in Respighi
a slow distant drumming
a distant thrumming
an insistent churning
as of many feet together turning
Along the Appian Way
among the dark pines and shattered shadows
in the dark day
as a red bird flies over
new legions coming
new legions marching
over the far horizon
through the dark trees
trumpets blaring
new flags unfurling
suddenly appearing
the closed ranks coming on
to the now-loud drums
the triumphant trumpets
brass horns and hollow bassos
ringing out
over the casqued warriors
the masked legionnaires
over the flashing columns
coming on and on
rank on rank
in new strange uniforms
no one has ever seen

CARRARA, LOOKING SEAWARD

Saw Carrara's marble mountains
   their great white faces
     open to the sea
Somewhere a voice was singing
          in sea caves off Saranza
  somewhere
      upon the white wind echoing
   far off
    in white stone sky
   Again . . .
        again . . .
            still echoing
     voce delirante
        figlia di mare
    Breasts of white marble
        Hair blown back
   aie
    aie
     che tanta bella luce
     della carne umana

AT THE *GARE BRUXELLES-MIDI*

Two people saying goodbye
but not saying it
Saying nothing
in the station at noon
in the *gare Bruxelles-Midi*
Not a word between them
They're both looking straight ahead
Their hands are clasped
on the cafe table
all four hands together
as in a children's hand game
Their hands are big
The man and the woman are not so big
They are grey and green
middle-aged
nondescript but distinguished
Even their skins seem grey
Il a l'air d'un petit fonctionnaire
a little bureaucrat somewhere
It is he who is taking the train
perhaps back to his wife in France
The woman here is a little younger
but far from young
Maybe he's French she's Belge
a wartime romance perhaps
Now forty years after
they're still meeting
across borders
Their four hands like the four wings of two doves
folded together
unable to fly away
from each other
Very capable hands
capable of a lot of things
but not of saying goodbye

not even of waving goodbye
Their hands are mute as mouths
He stands up now
He picks up
his heavy valise
He stands there still
She does not look up
He keeps standing there
looking nowhere
Then he walks away
All at once he walks away
around the corner out of sight
carrying his heavy valise
and his heavy briefcase
She does not look after him
She does not turn her head
She stares straight ahead
without blinking

A fly
walks
around
on the
table

TWO AMSTERDAMS

A voyage through the Low Countries
and tilted Amsterdam
like a barge in a bottle
a blown glass city
listing on its tides—
In the hotel café
they have rugs on the table
Dutch burghers munching mutton
while I sit here longing
          for the Transsiberian Express
       the wild taiga
              beyond Zima Station
    And the wide open spaces
              between Ship Rock and Taos
      high flat mesas like islands
             or ships adrift
                 in the desert
          Indians in undented
              black felt hats
    And prairies in sun
          seas of wheat in wind
              off the Great Lakes
    Or the running sea
          sweeping in
              off Cape Ann Gloucester
    Or the wild North Sea
            due North of here
          Vikings beating windward
               through the white nights
       Norwegians in open boats
             escaping the Nazis
No more macho heroes here
among the potted rubber plants!
      Yet not far away

throw-away heroes rocking onstage
at Paradiso dance hall
        Amsterdam Fillmore Auditorium
  stoned captain at the helm
     with stand-up mike swung like a sword
to the sound of sea crashing
        on splintered timber
  The deck quivers
    to the boomed electric beat
The ship tilts
   the crew roars
      in Liverpool accents
  the naked hero-bodies crash
       beyond the Milky Way
And in the blown-out dawn
     nudes struggle home
        through alleyways

THE LIVING THEATRE
(for Julian & Judith)

In a little side street
off the Museumplein
a lady talking on a telephone and crying
and staring out her secondfloor window
looks through me in the street

A block further on
a man looking down and smoking
and laughing in his telephone
looks through me invisible

The ground of the Rijksmuseum Park
is covered with sodden leaves
My footsteps
will leave no prints on them
But they and the people have left
their imprints in me
their distant emotions
fall on me as in
some tragic magic theatre

I do not laugh and cry with them
I am just their dramaturge
or some foreign theatre critic
come to see the spectacle
of their little lives played out

This show will never fold
no matter what the reviews
Tragedies will be tragedies
even if they laugh
The human comedy will still be comedy
even if not laughable
The show will go on
even if it's not Paradise Now
in the Living Theatre

EXPRESSIONIST HISTORY
OF GERMAN EXPRESSIONISM

The Blue Rider rode over The Bridge into the Bauhaus
on more than one blue horse
Franz Marc made his blue mark
on the blue scene
And Kirchner cantered through the dark circus
on a different dark horse
Emil Nolde never moldy danced boldly
around a golden calf
Max Pechstein fished in river landscapes
and fooled around with his models
(They all did that)
Rottluff painted his rusty lust
and Otto Mueller ate cruellers
as his painting got crueler
Erich Heckel heckled himself with madmen
and thereby foresaw their mad ends
Norwegian Munch let out a silent scream
Jawlensky made Matisse look mad and Russian
And Kandinsky grew insanely
incandescent
Kokoschka drew his own *sturm und drang*
Käthe Kollwitz chalked the face
of Death and the Mother
Schwitters twittered through trash cities
and Klee became a clay mobile
swaying to the strains of the Blue Angel
Otto Dix drew a dying warrior
on his steely palette
Grosz glimpsed the grossest
in the gathering storm
Max Beckmann saw the sinking of the Titanic
and Meidner painted the Apocalypse
Feininger traced a Tragic Being
and fingered skyscrapers

which fell across the Atlantic
(and the Bauhaus in its final antic
fell on Chicago)
Meanwhile back in Berlin
Hitler was painting himself
into a corner
And his ovens were heating
as a Tin Drum began beating

THE PHOTO OF EMILY

She wore a cloche hat
She was Aunt Emily
She spoke French She had a job
as a French governess
She stood on the bridge in Bronxville
over the Bronx River the little river
with its little woods and the little bridge
and the swimming hole and the woods
where we played Robin Hood
I thought I was Robin Hood
or one of his deerskin men
I wanted a deerskin suit
more than anything
I remember that clearly when I was eight
I stayed awake at night
thinking how to make it how to get it
I would have robbed a rich traveller
(That's how rebels are born)
She stood on the bridge in her hat
I came to her from the woods
where I'd been playing
by the little brown river
with its dirty crayfish
I came up to her
in her long lace dress and black pumps
She had elegant feet
long feet
an 'aristocrat's' she would say
She was a bit mad and compulsive
Even then I knew it
She was Catholic in a mad way
as if she had some special personal connection
with the Pope
She thought of herself as a writer
as having something special to say

in French
I thought of her as my French mother
She was my mother's French sister
the sister who'd been born in France
the family so mixed up
between Portugal and France
and the Virgin Islands
which was the route my mother's family took
to the United States
and Coney Island where the French kept
boardinghouses
and my mother met my father
when he came from Lombardy
speaking only Lombard
and ended up the first night
in that boardinghouse at Coney
My French mother Emily stands on the bridge
in the old photo
the only photo I had of her
A dark bridge and her face in shadow
Or perhaps her face was light once
and the photo darkened
There is a pearly strangeness
in the dark light
It is all I have of her
She must have had a box camera that day
I was wearing short pants
on that little stone bridge
(And who took the picture
of the two of us together
arms around each other?
So silent the old picture—
If it could only speak!)
It is her day off in the Nineteen Twenties
I am nine—
Where now
that elegant cloche hat
that woman lost in time

a shadowy strangeness is all
She had fine skin
gossamer hair
cut like Garbo
or Louise Brooks
but not so very beautiful
She had a wen on her breast
Might I not find that hat
and that woman still—
a seamstress in the back
of some small thrift shop—
Come back, come back—
At least the photo
might I not at least
find the photo again
in some lost album
with black cardboard pages
there's the photo
held on the stiff page
by little paper triangles pasted on
the photo of Emily
mad and elegant
thinking herself a great writer
with something to say to the world
in her shadow hat
having her picture taken
with the child she always wanted
She had lovers but no child
She stood by the bedside and took me
Life went on with us
The photo darkened
She was too distracted
too gypsy-like too self-willed
too obsessed too
passionately articulate
burning too bright
too much a lunatic of loving
to keep that child

who ran off finally
into the dark park of those days
by the Bronx River
and sees her now
nowhere else in memory
except by that dark bridge
And saw her never again
And never saw her again
except in the back of old boutiques
peered into now again
with haunting glance
in the Rue de Seine

LATE IMPRESSIONIST DREAM

In a late Impressionist dream I am riding in an open touring-car with a group of French women in summer dresses and picture hats with uncles in grey doeskin vests and striped shirts with armbands and everyone is laughing and chattering in French as if no other language had yet become socially accepted And we get to an outdoor cafe by the Seine on the outskirts of Paris as in a Manet painting under an arbor by the river drinking wine and eating a grand picnic out of wicker hampers And just then some loud young men drift by in punts on the river looking sheepishly like young American college students singing a drinking song about Whiffenpoofs and we go on talking French as if nothing else in the real world were happening anywhere And all the people around me turn into characters out of Marcel Proust and we are all in Swann's Way in a budding grove with a straight Odette chez Swann but then of a sudden Blaise Cendrars bursts in waving a newspaper headline screaming *"L'OR! L'OR!"* and gold has been discovered in California and I must leave immediately to join the Gold Rush and wake up in my cabin in Big Sur looking like a French Canuck Jack Kerouac and hearing the sound of the sea in which the fish still speak Breton

THE PLOUGH OF TIME

Night closed my windows and
The sky became a crystal house
The crystal windows glowed
The moon
shown through them
through the whole house of crystal
A single star beamed down
its crystal cable
and drew a plough through the earth
unearthing bodies clasped together
couples embracing
around the earth
They clung together everywhere
emitting small cries
that did not reach the stars
The crystal earth turned
and the bodies with it
And the sky did not turn
nor the stars with it
The stars remained fixed
each with its crystal cable
beamed to earth
each attached to the immense plow
furrowing our lives

THE REBELS

Star-stricken still
        we lie under them
             in dome of night
    as they wheel about
        in their revolutions
      forming and reforming
          their splendiferous
             phosphor fabrications

Ah the wheelwright of it
           (whoever he or she or it)
     chief fabricator
        of the night of it
      of the night to set it in
          this cut-glass
            diamond diagram

Upstairs
   in the lighted attic
      under the burning eaves
            of time
   lamps hung out
     (to guide far more far-out voyagers
       than ourselves)

Still antic stars
      shoot out
        burst out—
            errant rebels
      even there
    in the perfect pattern
        of some utopia
      shooting up
        tearing the
          silver web

As in a palm of hand
        the perfect plan of line
                of life and heart and head
    struck across of a sudden
              by one
                    cataclysmic tear

Yet all not asunder
             all not lost to darkness
    all held together still
               at some still center
        even now
      in the almost incendiary dawn
    as still another
            rebel burning bright
              strikes its match upon
                    our night

HISTORY OF THE WORLD:
A TV DOCU-DRAMA

Dark mind dark soul dark age
the peasant leads his horse
through blackberry kingdoms
and comes out at a crossroads
in North America
comes out on a highway
in the American West
the horse hitched to a prairie wagon
the ruts get wider
East of Santa Fe you can see from a plane
the old wagon trails in the earth
ruts a mile wide
you can almost hear
the crack of whips over horses
the cries of the drivers in the rising dust
The nineteenth century ends
and turns into Highway 66
prairie schooners into Pullmans
their dark saloons sheeted in oblivion
The myth haunts us
the rutting continues
The night of the horse is over
It is the dawn after dreaming
in the middle of the journey
we come upon our selves on a dark road
and recognize our selves for the first time
The lights come on
the country is electrified
the world lights up like a ferris wheel
All the machines begin to hum
almost in unison
Europa becomes a blind bull
hitched to an iron horse on rails
belching smoke

Civilization beats out Eros
and Proust perishes
Gauguin escapes to Tahiti
as Tristes Tropiques
perish forever
A crowd flows over London Bridge
Westward
stick figures in the world's end
out of Giacometti
The Golden Hinde sails through the Golden Gate
and sets up as a tourist attraction
Sir Francis Drake's brass plate is dug up
and ends up in a glass case
in Bancroft Library Berkeley
The Tower of London is sold
and transported to Texas
Easy Riders over the asphalt
roar stoned into the sunset
Stout Cortez still astounded on a peak
A Passage to India
and an empire collapses
as Spengler shouts 'I told you so!'
Chinese philosophers dreaming they are butterflies
drift up the Yangtse and disappear
as the sea continues its blind waves
Red tides reach up the Potomac
and paranoia floods the world
Drums drums drums Johnny Get Your Gun
In the morning still
a girl in a white linen dress
wearing a white picture hat
crosses Gatsby's lawn bright with promise
Gandhi dies but lives on
A Buddhist monk
immolates himself on-camera
Sri Ram Jai Ram Jai Jai Ram
Jesus on his Tree sticks up
on his horizon

signalling wildly
The rutting continues
'Strengthened to live Strengthened to die
for medals and positioned victories?'
'The world's an orphan's home'
Rootless polyglots roam the cities
spacecraft sweeping over
bearing short-haired Magellans in jumpsuits
as satellites sweep the earth
with high-resolution cameras
multiple fluid images
melding Minneapolis and Roumania
Mississippi and Krishna
Hari rama hari rama Rama rama hari hari
Fields and winds and waters
fog and birds and men
sweep the screen
and chase each other from it
The camera zooms in:
The Vietnam captain holds his pistol
to the peasant's head
It explodes in full color
on CBS ABC NBC
The world with its drums of blood
continues turning
The locust continues
to devour the world
Hunger persists
Love lurches on
listing to larboard
like a ship in a bottle
Human longing goes on
Loneliness a curse
Innocence persists
Ignorance persists
like a scratch on a TV window
like a scratch on a windshield
Twilight has no meaning

beyond the figurative
Europa rocks on the horizon
lights burning in the night
like the SS Queen Mary
tied up in Southern California
where the American Dream came too true
There is a soughing in the bilges
Somewhere a naive figure
holds up a laurel wreath
a nymph a valkyrie a sybil
holds up a Golden Bough
Lovers still are riders to the sea
A horse comes alone from a torn village
Ah love let us be true
to our selves
I'll put a note in a bottle
like a schooner in a bottle
it'll survive the worst seas
Turner's shipwreck burning
off the Hook of Holland
Friend, an albatross wings above our land
It's a bird It's a man It's a plane without wings
'Brightness falls from the air'
and the air burns
They used to call it a Darkling Plain
In the UN they are debating it
'It's still the same old story
a fight for love and glory'
A woman walks on the shore
Life still an inn of joy and sorrow
Beloved come back
by any bridge
Educated armies
march over it
In the twilight holding up her skirts
Anna Livia stands
on the far strand at ebb-tide
'swept with confused alarms'

An effect of Rembrandt
an effect of Turner
The air is shaken with light
the crickets begin again
on heavy summer nights
Somewhere in the snows
someone is beating a woman
A Russian poet records it
Boots begin
to march over it
The camera zooms in:
All the windows in every house in the world
turn into TV screens
all tuned to the same image
the image of children watching and waiting
watching a huge strange drifting cloud
Children are watching children waiting
The great cloud drifts ever closer and brighter
shaking the screen with shattered light
the broken light of modern painting
There's Nothing on the other channels
There's no sound
A child reaches up and turns up the volume
Still there's no sound
still there's only silence
still there's only the Ultimate Stillness
A child turns up the Brightness

INDEX

◆